CHINA BASICS SERIES

THE ARCHITECTURAL ART OF ANCIENT CHINA

Author: Lou Qingxi
Translator: Li Zhurun

2002.7

CHINA INTERCONTINENTAL PRESS

中国基本情况丛书

顾　　问　李　冰　赵少华

主　　编　郭长建

副 主 编　宋坚之(执行)　吴　伟

装帧设计　宁成春

本册责任编辑　冯凌宇

图书在版编目(CIP)数据

中国传统建筑／楼庆西著，－北京：五洲传播出版社，2001.2
ISBN 7－80113－822－8

Ⅰ.中…
Ⅱ.楼…
Ⅲ.建筑艺术－中国－古代－英文
Ⅳ.TU－092

五洲传播出版社出版发行

北京北三环中路31号　邮政编码 100088

HTTP：//WWW.CICC.ORG.CN

＊

2001年10月第1版　第1次印刷
889×1194毫米 32开 5.5印张 47千字
004500

TABLE OF CONTENTS

A Summary of Ancient China's Archifectural Art

China, one of the most ancient countries in the world, has a history of more than 5,000 years. At the mention of the Chinese civilization, its architectural achievements in particular, we customarily call to mind monuments like the Great Wall, the Forbidden City and the Temple of Heaven. As we see them, these structures indeed represent the essence of traditional Chinese architecture. But it has to be noted that other ancient structures in countless numbers can also be found on the vast land of China. To name just some: cities and towns of classical beauty, imposing palace complexes, magnificent tombs and mausoleums, awe-inspiring temples and altars, gardens that feature a harmony of natural and artificial beauty, and residential buildings beautiful with a primitive simplicity. These provide ample material evidence to the development of the Chinese civilization over the milleniums. Whatever it is, an ancient structure enlivens the spirit of China's traditional culture and, in one way or another, represents ancient China's accomplishments in construction techniques and architectural art.

Of the numerous schools of architectural art in the world, the Chinese school of architectural art strikes a line for itself. What are its most salient features? Here is a summary:

Wooden framing is the basic feature of ancient Chinese structures

Ancient Egyptians had to their credit those pyramids, and ancient Greece and Rome built those pits, arches and temples. These are all stone structures. In comparison, ancient Chinese structures, ranging from a simple residential building to a magnificent palace hall or a mausoleum, are mostly built with timber. The process of construction was basically the same. The first step was to erect some wooden columns on the foundation. Then wooden beams and bulks were fixed on the

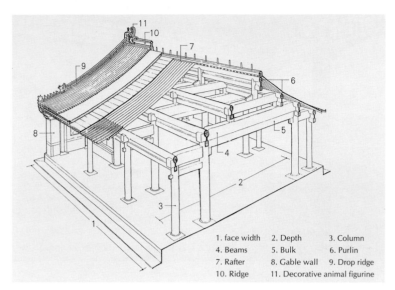

1. face width	2. Depth	3. Column
4. Beams	5. Bulk	6. Purlin
7. Rafter	8. Gable wall	9. Drop ridge
10. Ridge	11. Decorative animal figurine	

Diagrammatic sketch of the structural framing of an ancient Chinese building.

columns, which, together with the purlins, would form the frame of the roof. The last step was to lay tiles on the frame of the roof. Walls of bricks or rammed earth were built at the same time, round the columns. It has to be noted that the upright columns, not the walls, are the supporting parts of the building, hence the old saying, "walls may collapse, houses – never."

Wooden frame structures were popular for a variety of reasons. In the first place, materials for constructing such structures were easily available and the construction methods were relatively simple. Ancient China had abundant forest resources, and felling of trees was certainly easier than quarrying. Through centuries of practice, ancient Chinese architects and workmen developed a modularized system for construction. To put it in plain language, the system called for using a key part of the wooden structure as the standard or as the basic unit of measurement, by which the architect would decide, through computation, the proper sizes of the columns, beams, purlins, doors and windows. Then workmen would build the different parts of the structure according to the prescribed sizes and standards, which they

Wooden frame structures without walls - waterside pavilions, corridors, etc.

pieced together on the construction site at a later stage. This way of doing things made it possible for construction to proceed despite adverse weather conditions and other natural odds. A striking example is the construction of the Forbidden City that began in 1407 under the third emperor of the Ming Dynasty (1368-1644). It took just 13 years for the entire complex - nearly 1,000 halls, chambers and gardens in an area of 720,000 square meters - to be completed. In contrast, it took Italian workers nearly 30 years to complete just the grand stone dome of the Florenze Cathedral. Secondly, wooden frame structures are safer in earthquakes. The different parts of a wooden frame structure are connected with joggles and mortise joints. The flexibility of the joggles and mortises, plus the strength of the timber, helps prevent the structure from breaking up or collapsing when a strong tremor strikes. In Yingxian County, Shanxi Province, there is a wooden Buddhist pagoda built 900 years ago. The structure has remained intact even though several strong earthquakes have struck the area since it was built. Thirdly, as we have mentioned, walls are not the supporting parts of a wooden frame structure. And because of this, walls can be built in ways that best suit local conditions. In north China where it is cold, structures normally have thick, solid walls. In south China where it is hot, walls of houses are often built with wooden boards or woven bamboo mats. There are even structures without walls, such as *ting* (pavilions), *xie* (pavilions on terraces), *lang* (corridors) and some of the halls we find in traditional gardens and scenic spots. Moreover, a large room may easily be partitioned into chambers with wooden boards or screens. Solid walls can, of course be built to partition the room if its owner likes it.

But wooden frame structures are not as strong as brick or stone structures. Few ancient buildings of wooden frame structure have remained intact to this day because timber is easy to burn and become moth-eaten or rotten. In fact countless ancient buildings of wooden frame structure were destroyed in fires caused by lightning. The Hall of Supreme Harmony, the most important structure in the Forbidden City, was destroyed this way the year after it was built. In the following centuries, it was destroyed again and again in fires, and again and again it was rebuilt.

Ground plan of ancient structures

A neat cluster of buildings that form a Buddhist temple on the back of the Longevity Hill in the Summer Palace.

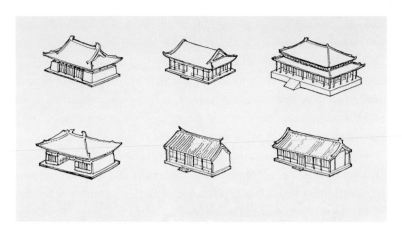

Roofs in different forms denote differences in ranking between the occupiers.

In most cases, ancient Chinese structures are in neat groups or clusters, whether they are palace complexes, temples or residential buildings. Few ancient Chinese structures have so complicated a plane layout and so imposing an outlook as those cathedrals and mansions in the West, but in groups or clusters they look equally magnificent, if not more. Just take residential buildings, for example. In north China, *si he yuan* are the most popular housing buildings in traditional style. A *si he yuan* is a rectangular compound formed with four neat rows of one-story rooms of gray tiles and bricks. The head of the family and his wife occupy the room in the middle of the row facing south, which is flanked by rooms for junior members of the family on either side. In most cases the rooms are not really large, but as a group, they are sufficient to satisfy the needs of all family members.

Wall led compounds like *si he yuan* are, in fact, typical of all ancient Chinese structures in terms of ground plan or plane layout. In other words, palace complexes and temples are much the same as *si he yuan*, the difference being that the former are much larger, consisting of courtyards and building not only greater in numbers but also more requisitely decorated. Rooms with four columns as the supporting parts are the basic units for ancient Chinese wooden frame structures. Several rooms built together form an independent row, and it is rows of rooms that form compounds or courtyards, large or small. A city in ancient China was, as a matter of fact, formed with clusters of compounds and courtyards serving different purposes.

Buildings in neat clusters or groups that form compounds or courtyards represent the predominant artistic pattern for traditional Chinese structures. But it has to be remembered that traditional Chinese structures are diverse in style and plane layout. In mountainous and other areas with complicated landforms, people have had to take into full account of the local topographical conditions in planning the layout of the different structures in a compound. In such places, structures,

Decorative figurines on the roof of a Buddhist temple in Yunnan Province.

compounds and courtyards do not necessarily feature a bilateral symmetry. In south China, for example, clusters of residential buildings with and without courtyards can both be found.

The principle for design and construction of gardens of classical style can be summarized as "attainment of natural beauty by means of

The roof (partial) of a building in the Forbidden City, Beijing.
Pay attention to the decorative pattern.

painstaking human labor", which aims at creating landscapes producing a variety of visual effects. In other words, bilateral symmetry that characterizes traditional courtyards and compounds does not apply to classical gardens. Meanwhile, it needs to be noted that buildings in mountainous areas and classical gardens are not independent of themselves. Instead, such buildings are integral parts of a given architectural complex.

Artistic treatment of traditional Chinese structures

Exteriors of traditional Chinese structures are invariably decorated for artistic effects. To be precise, the entire buildings are decorated along with their exposed parts such as eaves, tiles and beams. When building a structure, ancient Chinese always worked painstakingly to make everything in its exterior -- even those eaves and tiles -- highly decorative. The roof of a typical ancient building is, in fact, an elaborate system of wooden beams and purlins and, as such, it may look heavy. But in no way does it look clumsy as the four tips curve up. Through centuries of practice, Chinese workmen and engineers developed ways to ensure that the roof of a structure assumes the form commensurate with the purpose of the structure or the its owner's social status.

Moreover, the various construction members of the ridgepole are invariably in the shape of small animals, and floral and animal designs are carved even on those tile-ends, making the entire building look even more enchanting. To prolong the life of a building, the exposed parts of the eaves and purlins are invariably painted, culminating in a unique art form known as *cai hua* or decorative paintings. Besides, carvings are always done on the stone terrace of an ancient structure, as well as its wooden windows and brick doors.

Such decorations are beautiful, carrying a great deal of cultural messages. The Chinese have always seen the legendary dragon and phoenix as auspicious. Besides, in ancient times the dragon and phoenix were associated to the imperial power, and were taken as the "logos" of the emperor and the queen, respectively. That explains why so many imperial buildings left over from the past are decorated with dragon and phoenix designs and patterns. The Chinese also regard some other animals as auspicious, as their names and certain auspicious words are homophonic. One best example is the bat. The characters 福 (happiness) and 蝠 (bat) are homonyms, both pronounced as "fu". Just for that, the

Decorative patterns of dragons, clouds and spirals painted on the beam of a building in the Forbidden City, Beijing.

bat is seen as an auspicious animal and often appears in folk paintings and handicraft articles. Windows of traditional housing buildings are often decorated with a pattern of five bats forming a circle round the character 寿 (pronounced as "shou", meaning "long life"). There are also animals and birds seen as auspicious for being symbolic or their natural characteristics. The tortoise, for example, is taken as a symbol of long life because it does live long. Mandarin ducks are the very embodiment of love, of mutual loyalty cherished by a couple, because the male and female birds in a pair are often seen "fondling" each other with their pecks, reminiscent of the husband and wife intoxicated with love. Natural characteristics of plants can be used to refer to people's social characteristics. For their elegance and luxuriant beauty, peony is referred to as the "queen of all flowers" and seen as the symbol of riches and honor. The pine and cypress are evergreen and always stand erect in defiance of wind and snow, thus seen as a symbols of strength, willpower and moral integrity. In addition to auspicious and symbolic animals, birds and plants, historic figures and stories are often the themes of decorative patterns painted or carved on traditional structures. To sum up, decorative patterns and designs, in their own ways, enlivens the cultural side of the Chinese nation while adding artistic beauty to traditional structures.

Ever since its birth, the Chinese nation has comprised numerous ethnic groups. In the 1950s, work was done to identify the different ethnic groups living in the country. And in the following decade, nationwide investigations were made into the history and society of each ethnic minority group. The country has 56 ethnic groups. The ethnic Han people are the majority, accounting for 93% of the national population. Over the milleniums, the various ethnic groups have together built up the brilliant Chinese culture through exchange and communication. Meanwhile, each ethnic group has been able to retain its own cultural identity. Structures of the ethnic Tibetans are a strong expression of the Tibetan school of Buddhism. Though some artistic techniques of the Hans are used in their construction, ethnic Tibetan structures are imposing in outlook, bright in color and beautiful with a primitive simplicity. The Uygurs are proud of their architectural accomplishments in Islamic style which, as an independent architectural system in China, are simple and vigorous enough to create an artistic conception of magnificence and tranquility. The ethnic Dai people living in Yunnan Province, southwest China, believe in the Sthaviravada school of Buddhism, hence the similarity between religious shrines there and those in Myanmar and Thailand where the same school of Buddhism dominates.

Structures of the Han ethnic majority are the mainstream of China's traditional architectural art. Meanwhile, it has to be remembered that all the minority ethnic groups have contributed to the development of traditional Chinese architecture. Now we' like to provide a brief account of traditional structures which, according to conventional methods for classification of ancient buildings, fall into the categories of palace structures, altars and temples, religious structures, tombs and mausoleums, gardens and residential buildings.

Palace Structures

The story goes back to the year 206 BC when Liu Bang, leader of the most powerful peasant rebel army, overthrew the tyrannical Qin Dynasty (221 BC - 206 BC), established a new Dynasty which he chose to call "Han", and named himself "Emperor Gao Zu". Immediately after the new Dynasty was inaugurated in Chang'an (what is now Xi'an of Shaanxi Province), his ministers and generals proposed that a large palace complex be built for him. The new emperor, however, was hesitant, knowing that so much needed to be done as the country was far from being pacified. "Why is it that we should use so huge an amount of financial and human resources on such a thing when the country is still in turmoil?" he asked Xiao He, his prime minister. Xiao He, legendary for wisdom, replied: "The Son of Heaven reigns supreme over all land within the Four Seas. His majesty's might won't be known to his subjects if he does not have an imposing enough palace complex."

The story is sufficient to suggest that while serving the imperial needs for accommodation and work, palace structures were symbolic of the imperial might and power, the supremacy of the emperors. That explains why throughout China's history of feudalism, the founding emperor of any dynasty would spare no effort to have a magnificent palace complex built for himself. The best architects, engineers and workmen would be called in for the job, and the best materials available in the country would be used. That is why the palace structures were always the largest and the best in quality, representing the highest achievements made under the dynasty in architectural art and construction engineering.

China's Palace Structures through the Centuries

Far back in the 21st century BC, the Xia, the first dynasty in China, came into being. On order of the Xia rulers, walls were built round the capital city, along with palaces in it.

The Xia was to be replaced by the Shang Dynasty (16th century BC - 11th century BC). According to historic records, before it overturned the Xia, the Shang Dynasty had moved its capital six times before it settled it in Yin (what is now Anyang City, Henan Province). Archeological excavation and textual research have resulted in the discovery that the dynasty's palace complex consists of three zones, the north, central and south, with the north and central zones probably reserved for accommodation and work of the top rulers while serving as the venues of religious and sacrificial ceremonies. Based on their study of the ruins of some 50 foundations, experts have concluded that palace structures of the Shang Dynasty must have been built on raised

Restored map of the Delin Hall in the Daming Palace of the Tang Dynasty.

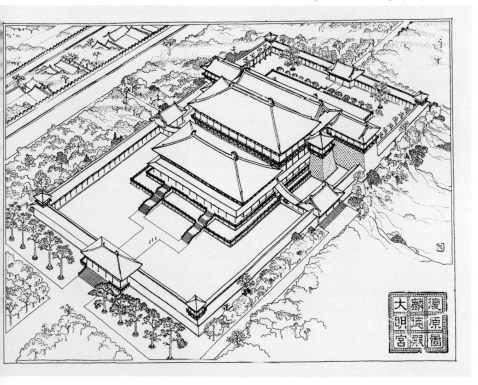

A part of the roof of a hall in the Forbidden City.

A bird's-eye-view of the Forbidden City.

earthen platforms about one meter high, and that the largest structure was 80 meters long and 14.5 meters wide.

The succeeding Zhou Dynasty (11th century BC - 256 BC) made Gao (somewhere to the southwest of Xi'an City, Shaanxi Province) its capital and then moved it to Luoyi (what is now Luoyang City, Henan Province). The two sites are yet to be excavated. According to the *Artificers' Record*, the sixth part of the *Ritual of Zhou*, the Zhou Dynasty's capital was a walled square, with three grates on each side of the wall. The palace complex was a cluster of structures in the central part of the city. The structures were in three neat rows, and in their front there were five gates.

In 221 BC, Emperor Shi Huang of the

Qin Dynasty unified China. By then feudalism had established itself in China and, thanks to better developed productive forces, Emperor Shi Huang - literally meaning the "first emperor" - was able to build for himself a palace complex unprecedented in size and extravagance in the capital, Xianyang, or Xi'an of the present day. The Efang Palace, the principal structure in the palace complex, was 150 meters wide and had a front as long as 300 meters. Round the palace there was a long corridor leading to the foot of Mt. Nanshan, a range of rolling hills presumably serving as the palace's *que* towers[1]. Construction of the palace complex was half done when the Qin Dynasty was overthrown.

Feudalism experienced its heyday during the Tang Dynasty (618-907). The dynasty's capital, Chang'an (what is now Xi'an), was the world's largest city. Development of the city was painstakingly planned. The palace structures were initially in the so-called "Imperial City"

that occupied the northern part of the capital. Later on, an even larger palace complex, the Daming Palace, was built outside the city. The Daming Palace was a neat compound, with the main buildings standing at either side of its axis. In front of the Hanyuan Hall, the principal hall, there was a road leading to the main gate of the compound and, at either side of hall, there was a neat row of less important halls. The magnificence

A bronze vase in the Forbidden City. It was used to hold water for fire fighting.

of the palace structures testified to China's might and prosperity under the Tang Dynasty.

In 1279, the Mongols set up the Yuan Dynasty, which was to reign supreme over the country until 1368. The dynasty was the first national regime set up by an ethnic minority group of China's. In following the tradition, the founding rulers of the dynasty built for themselves a palace complex in the capital, Dadu - the "Great Capital" — or what is now Beijing. The "Imperial City" and the "Palace City"[2] were in the center of the capital. The main palace structures stood in order of bilateral symmetry, astride the north-south axis of the Palace City.

Unfortunately, none of the palace structures built under the Yuan and earlier dynasties is preserved. The Forbidden City in Beijing, the largest and best-preserved palace complex in the world, was home to the imperial families of the Ming (1368-1644) and Qing dynasties (1644-1911). Also well, preserved is the Qing Imperial Palace in Shenyang, northeast China, which was built before the Manchurians unified China. The Forbidden City of Beijing, however, is seen as the best example of China's palace structures.

Palace structures built under different dynasties differ in size. Meanwhile, palace structures of all dynasties have a lot in common. In the first place, such structures are independent of one another, each designed to serve a specific imperial need - for handling of state and court affairs, accommodation, rest and recreation, or conducting of religious and sacrificial activities. Secondly, these individual structures form a neat group according to stringent patriarchal rules that were passed down from one dynasty to the next. The main structures invariable sit astride the north-south axis of the palace compound, flanked by less important buildings in order of bilateral symmetry. Buildings in the frontal part of the palace compound were reserved for the handling of court affairs and the imperial living quarters were in the rear part, along with the imperial garden. Thirdly, walls surround this neat group of palace structures, forming the so-called "palace city" that normally lies in the central part of the capital city. All feudal dynasties followed this

A partial view of the stone platform, on which the Forbidden City's "Three Great Halls" stand.

The "imperial avenue" leading to the Hall of Preservation of Harmony, one of the "Three Great Halls" in the Forbidden City. It is in fact a single piece of stone that is 16 meters long, three meters wide and 1.7 meters thick, and weighs 250 tons. Nine dragons are carved on it.

fixed pattern in planning the plane layout of their palace complexes.

The Forbidden City of Beijing

The Forbidden City of Beijing was the power center of China's last two feudal dynasties, the Ming and the Qing, which ruled China for altogether 491 years, from 1421 to 1911. All in all, 13 Ming emperors and 11 Qing emperors were housed in the Forbidden City, the largest and the best-preserved palace complex in China and the world. And as such, it represents the highest achievements ancient China was able to make in architectural engineering and art.

Farm back in 1045 BC, the City of Yan was built in what is now Beijing. In 1153 AD, the Jin Dynasty, a political regime set up by an ethnic minority group that ruled parts of north China, made the City of Yan its capital and gave it the new name "Zhong Du" - the "central capital". This marked the beginning for Beijing to serve as capital of political regimes, either local or national. It was on the basis of the "central capital" that in the 13th century, the founding emperors of the Yuan Dynasty started developing Beijing as the national capital, which they chose to call "Da Du" - the "great capital".

Construction of the Forbidden City

In 1386, peasant rebel armies under the command of Zhu Yuanzhang toppled the rule of the Mongols over China and one more feudal dynasty, the Ming, came into being, with what is now Nanjing as capital. Zhu Yuanzhang, who named himself Emperor Tai Zu of the Ming Dynasty, sent his more than two dozen sons to different parts of China, investing in them hereditary titles and territories. Zhu Di, Zhu Yuanzhang's fourth son, was the most powerful - also the most resourceful and the most ambitious - of the princes. He was named Prince Yan, and sent to Beijing, where he managed to build up a private army. After Zhu Yuanzhang died, Zhu Yunwen, the eldest male child of the eldest son born of his

Picture shows one of the four turrets atop the four
corners of the wall that surrounds the Forbidden City.

crown empress, was made the new emperor - Emperor Jian Wen as known to historians. Shortly after the new emperor was enthroned, Prince Yan in Beijing started an armed rebellion, pronouncedly to "rid the emperor of those evil ministers round him". In 1402, Zhu Di's troops stormed into Nanjing, and Emperor Jian Wen went missing. The same year saw Zhu Di, or Prince Yan, make himself emperor. Immediately afterwards, the new emperor, Emperor Yong Le, decided to move the capital to Beijing, his old power base, in part to strengthen the defense against invasion of north China by people of ethnic minority groups from further north.

Construction of the Forbidden City began in 1406. The first thing that had to be done was to get the building materials. Most ancient Chinese buildings were wooden structures. To construct the Forbidden City, large quantities of timber - in fact timber of the highest quality - would be needed. Timber used in construction of the Forbidden City was mostly produced in south China, in Zhejiang, Jiangxi, Hunan and Hubei provinces, and water transport was virtually the sole means to get it to the north. It often took three or four years for the process to complete, from felling of trees to letting the trunks drift eastward in the Yangtze River and then northward in the Grand Canal that connects Hangzhou in the south and Beijing in the north.

Also needed were huge quantities of bricks, and the quality standards were especially demanding for floor bricks. Floor bricks were made of a special kind of clay through firing, and an elaborate process was followed in their production. The first step was to soak the clay in water and then carefully screen it to get rid of the alien matters in it. The second step was the firing of the bats. Bricks fresh from the kilns would be polished and then soaked in tung oil. The finished products were referred to as "gold bricks" as they were hard and smooth and, when struck, were able to produce a sound as pleasant to the ear as music from a metal repercussion instrument. "Gold bricks" were produced mainly in Suzhou of Jiangsu Province, and were shipped to Beijing along the Grand Canal.

Stone materials were also needed in huge quantities, for roads and

Plan of the Forbidden City.

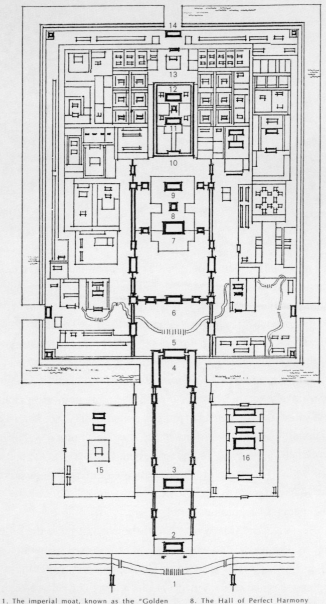

1. The imperial moat, known as the "Golden Water River", outside the Forbidden City.
2. The Gate of Heavenly Peace
3. The Gate of Correct Demeanor
4. The Meridian Gate
5. The section of the imperial moat inside the Forbidden City.
6. The Gate of Supreme Harmony
7. The Hall of Supreme Harmony
8. The Hall of Perfect Harmony
9. The Hall of Preservation of Harmony
10. The Gate of Heavenly Purity
11. The Palace of Heavenly Purity
12. The Hall of Earthly Tranquility
13. The Imperial Garden
14. The Gate of of Divine Prowess
15. Altar of the Land and Grain
16. Temple of Imperial Ancestors

The Meridian Gate, the south gate of the Forbidden City.

the huge platform on which the "Three Great Halls" were to be built. Rocks were available in areas round Beijing, but just for their weight, stone materials were no less difficult to transport than timber and bricks. The "Imperial Avenne", a carved stone in front of the Hall of Preservation of Harmony, the heaviest of all stones used in construction of the Forbidden City, is 16 meters long, three meters wide and 1.7 meters thick, and weighs 250 tons. Remember that this is just the weight of a single rock after processing! How so big and heavy a thing was transported to the construction site when everything had to be done manually? The job was done in the dead of winter. As the first step, workmen dug wells along the road from the quarry to the construction site, and sprayed water from the wells on the surface of the road. When the road surface was frozen, workmen would find it easier to move heavy things forward on it.

Bright yellow glazed tiles had to be used to build the roofs of the imperial structures. To meet the needs for glazed tiles, kilns were set up in several places in Beijing. The Liulichang Street in downtown Beijing was one of such places, "Liulichang" literally meaning "kiln of glazed tiles". Like Liulichang, the names of many other places originated from construction of the Forbidden City: Damucang (the "large timber yard"), an alley in Xichang District, Fangzhuan ("floor bricks"), an alley near the Drum Tower, etc. According to historic records, the "large timber yard" or "Damucang" was indeed large - "3, 000 times the size of an ordinary room".

It took whole ten years for workmen to get all the materials ready for the construction of the Forbidden City. In 1417, work began to build the Forbidden City. On order of Emperor Yong Le, more than 100,000 skilled laborers were press-ganged to Beijing from all over the country, along with unskilled workers who were several times as many. The Forbidden City occupies an area of 720,000 square meters, and has more than 1,000 buildings with a total of 9,000 rooms. It may be interesting to note that its construction was completed in just three years. In 1420, Emperor Yong Le came to settle in the Forbidden City, and Beijing officially became the national capital.

Ground Plans of Beijing and the Forbidden City

As the national capital of the Ming Dynasty, Beijing was built on the basis of what had been done in the previous dynasty, the Yuan. To

The north side of the Meridian Gate.

understand the ground plan of old Beijing, it might be convenient to think of it as consisting of three enclosures, each inside another. The innermost enclosure was the "Palace City", that is, the Forbidden City. Beyond the Forbidden was the "Imperial City" with Tian'enmen, the Gate of Heavenly Peace, as its main gate. And beyond the Imperial City lies the capital city itself. High walls used to enclose the capital city, which altogether had nine gates with magnificent watchtowers atop. But in the most recent decades, the walls have been dismantled for additional construction space as the city expands, and the only things left intact are a few short, separate sections and the South-Facing Gate, the south gate for the old capital city. In 1533, work began to build a wall round the capital city to strengthen Beijing's defense. The project came to a halt after construction was completed on the south section of the wall. So the capital city came to be known as the "inner city", while the part to the south of the capital city was referred to as the "outer city".

Now let's examine the ground plan of Beijing during the Ming and Qing dynasties. A road runs straight from south to north through the city, forming the longitudinal axis along which the city was planned. The road starts at the Gate of Perpetual Peace, the south gate of the "outer city", and runs to the South-Facing Gate, the central gate of the "inner city". Lying to the east of the south section of the road is the Temple of Heaven, where the emperors worshipped Heaven in whose name they ruled China; and to the west, the Altar of the God of Agriculture, where the emperors offered sacrifices and begged for good harvests. In between the South-Facing Gate and the Gate of Heavenly Peace there used to be the Imperial Road, a wide, straight road paved with slab stones, and running parallel to the road was a long corridor at either side, beyond which there were office buildings of the various ministries.

Here we are, in the compound in between the Gate of Heavenly Peace, the main gate of the Imperial City, and the Meridian Gate, the south gate of the Forbidden City. Beyond either side of the road linking the two gates there stands a neat road of one-story buildings where

The Gate of Supreme Harmony, the gate of the Forbidden City's frontal part where emperors of the Ming and Qing dynasties handled state affairs.

court ministers gathered for imperial audiences. Walking through the Meridian Gate we find ourselves inside the Forbidden City. After visiting those magnificent halls we reach the north gate of the Forbidden City, the Gate of Divine Prowess. Facing the Gate of Divine Prowess across the street is the Prospect Hill. A pavilion sits atop the hill, which is the commanding height of Beijing. Straight to the north of the hill lies the north gate of the Imperial City, the Gate of Earthly Peace. Lying further north are the Bell Tower and the Drum Tower, from which time had been told day after day until after China became a republic in 1911. The city's longitudinal axis runs straight for 7,500 meters, from the Gate of Perpetual Peace to the Bell Tower, along which all buildings, including those in the Forbidden City, were planned. The ground plan of Beijing, in itself, brings to light the will of the emperors to rule from the center, reigning supreme over the entire China.

The Forbidden City is, indeed, the center of the city. It is 961 meters from south to north and 753 meters from east to west, surrounded by crimson walls ten meters high. Beyond the wall there is the moat, which is 52 meters wide. Each side of the walled palace complex has a gate. Atop each corner of the wall there stands a turret. While serving as sentry posts, the four turrets, mirrored in the moat, add beauty to the Forbidden City.

The frontal part of the Forbidden City was where the Ming and Qing emperors handled court affairs. The rear part was reserved as the living quarters of the emperors and their families. The "Three Great Halls", namely, the Hall of Supreme Harmony, the Hall of Perfect Harmony and the Hall of Preservation of Harmony, are the main structures in the frontal part of the Forbidden City. These were the venues of important ceremonies and, as such, sit astride the longitudinal axis of the Forbidden City. Lying to the east of the Three Great Halls is the imperial studio, known as the Hall of Literary Glory; and to the west, the Hall of Military Prowess, where the emperors gave audience to individual court ministers, and did fasting before attending sacrificial ceremonies.

In the rear part of the Forbidden City, there are structures serving the varied needs of the emperors in work and every day life. There are chambers where the emperors handled routine affairs of the state,

The Meridian Gate seen from the Gate of Supreme Harmony.

Bronze lion in front of the Gate of Supreme Harmony.

housing buildings for members of the imperial families, halls for Buddha worshipping and other religious activities, as well as the Imperial Garden. Nevertheless, only a few most important halls sit astride the longitudinal axis of the Forbidden. These include the Hall of Heavenly Purity, the bedchamber of the Emperor and his crown empress, and Hall of Earthly Tranquility, the imperial nuptial chamber. Structures at either side of the axis include the Six West Halls that housed the queen mother and concubines of the previous emperor, and the Six East Halls where concubines of the reigning emperor lived. The "Five East Chambers" and the "Five West Chambers" were the living quarters of the crown prince.

Numerous buildings are enclosed in the Forbidden City, either in its frontal or rear part. Buildings serving the same imperial need are grouped in separate courtyards, forming neat clusters that flank the longitudinal axis in order of bilateral symmetry and are connected by a web of roads.

Major structures in the Forbidden City

The Meridian Gate: This is the south gate of the Forbidden City. Its front has a wing at either side, and the structure therefore assumes the shape of ⌒. The front and its wings are, in fact, a raised platform some

10 meters high, and atop the front there is a hall with a nine-bay front. Atop either of the wing there is a neat row of one-story buildings that extend southward, with a square pavilion standing at eiither end. The Meridian Gate is 37.95 meters high, measured from the ground to the ridge of the hall atop its front, taller than any other Forbidden City structure. Besides, it is of the highest status among the same kind of structures found anywhere in the country.

The Meridian Gate has five gates, three in the front and one in either of the wings. The gate in the middle was reserved for the emperor. The crown empress was allowed to enter the middle gate once in her life - when she went inside the Forbidden City for wedding. The top three winners in court examination[3] may pass through the middle gate when they left the Forbidden City. Like the crown empress, they were given the honor only once in their lives. Imperial princes and court ministers were allowed to pass through the east and west gates when entering the Forbidden City for imperial audiences and leaving afterwards. The "side gates" in the wings were opened only for court examinations and for gatherings of all imperial princes and court ministers, the east "side gate" for use by civil officials and the west "side gates", for use by military officials. As regards those to attend court examination, their entrance and exit of the Forbidden City were arranged according to their positions in the final examination for officialdom. The east side gate was reserved for those whose positions were in single numbers, and the west side gate, for those whose positions were in round numbers.

While the main entrance of the Forbidden City, the Meridian Gate served a range of ceremonial purposes. After returning from war, the victorious imperial troops would parade in front of the Meridian Gate to be reviewed by the emperor sitting on the Gate, and showed him the prisoners of war they had taken back. Imperial decrees were read out from atop the Meridian Gate to a crowd of court ministers who gathered below. The Meridian Gate was also the venue of the ceremony marking the publication of a new version of the Imperial Calendar. As a routine, the emperor called court meetings on the fifth, 15th and 25th days of every month. If one day the emperor did not want or was unable to

The Hall of Supreme Harmony, the tallest structure in the Forbidden City.

attend the court meeting, the imperial princes may leave but the court ministers were obliged to stay outside the Meridian Gate, in case the emperor would want any of them in. In the Ming Dynasty, court ministers could be flogged for having invoked displeasure of his majesty. The imperial order for having a minister punished this way was invariably executed in front of the Meridian Gate.

The Gate of Supreme Harmony: Here we are in the frontal part of the Forbidden City, after walking through the Meridian Gate. The Gate of Supreme Harmony stands majestically before us. Behind it we'll find the "Three Great Halls". In between the Meridian Gate and the Gate of Supreme Harmony there is a compound as large as 26,000 square meters. The Golden Water River, in fact an artificial stream that curves like a jade belt, flows through the south part of the compound. Across the river there are five bridges of pure white marble. Ancient Chinese believed in geomancy, the assumption that the location of a house or a tomb and its natural surroundings were bound to influence

the family's fortune. In their opinion, a house or a tomb should, most ideally, have a hill behind, so that it would be protected from wind. In front of the house or tomb there should be a river or stream flowing by, because a reliable source of water, it was believed, was vital to the family's prosperity. It is exactly this belief that prompted builders of the Forbidden City to dig the Golden Water River. The "river", so to speak, diverts water from the moat outside the northwest corner of the Forbidden City, passes by some important imperial structures as it flows, and empties into the moat outside the southeast corner of the Forbidden City. While mainly symbolic, it nonetheless serves as the source of water for fire fighting and drains off rainwater.

The Gate of Supreme Harmony stands majestically in the middle of the compound's north part. This is a complicated structure that looks exactly like a palace hall, the main gate being flanked by two smaller gates. Unlike the Meridian Gate with a tower on a wall of three sides, the Gate of Supreme Harmony sits on a pure white marble platform and has no wings, suggesting that it is lower in status. Two bronze lions guard the Gate of Supreme Harmony, adding glory to the structure. The Chinese regard the lion as the "king of all animals" for its strength and fierceness. For this reason, the residence of a powerful family invariably had a lion and a lioness, of either stone or bronze, at its gate. The lion is always seen playing with a ball in its paws, and the lioness, fondling with her cubs.

While the main gate of the frontal part of the Forbidden City, the Gate of Supreme Harmony served as a venue where emperors worked on court affairs. In the Ming Dynasty, court ministers were obliged to gather at the gate early in the morning every day, waiting for imperial orders or audience from his majesty. If the reigning emperor happened to be hardworking, he would, intermittently, join the court ministers for discussion or to issue orders. The practice, known as "court meetings at the Imperial Gate", continued into the succeeding dynasty, the Qing,

Interior of the Hall of Supreme Harmony. Pay attention to the dragon throne in the middle.

and the only difference was that the Gate of Heavenly Purity was made the venue. Emperor Kang Xi (1662-1722), one of feudal China's greatest statesmen and military strategists, was present most frequently at "court meetings at the Imperial Gate". The succeeding emperors, however, were not so hardworking - in fact each being lazier than the preceding one. The practice was dropped in 1861, after the outbreak of the Second Opium War in which China suffered a humuliating defeat.

The Hall of Supreme Harmony: Now that we are in the frontal part of the Forbidden City, we find ourselves in a square even larger than the square in between the Meridian Gate and the Gate of Supreme Harmony. High on a pure white marble platform in the north of the 30, 000-square meter square stand the "Three Great Halls" - the Hall of Supreme Harmony, the Hall of Perfect Harmony and the Hall of Preservation of Harmony. Ancient Chinese buildings are mostly wooden structures and, as such, were often built on raised platforms as a precaution against damage by humidity. As time went by, the raised platform supporting a building became a major indicator of the building's status. The platform on which the Three Great Halls sit is a three-story structure some 8.17 meters high, indicating that it is higher in status than any other structures of the kind.

The Hall of Supreme Harmony is the most important structure in the Forbidden City. It was the venue for the most important ceremonies. New emperors were enthroned and their crown empresses appointed in the hall, which was also the venue for ceremonies celebrating the emperor's wedding and birthday and ceremonies for declaration of war by the emperor on behalf of the country. On the Spring Festival and other most important festivals, the emperor, sitting on the dragon throne high up in the center of the hall, would receive greetings from imperial princes and court ministers. After that, he would honor them at a banquet in the same hall.

For its importance, the Hall of Supreme Harmony is larger and more lavishly decorated than the other two "great halls". It has an 11-bay front, 60.01 meters long, and is a five-bay or 33.33 meters wide, and measured 35.05 meters from the ground to its ridge. It is, in fact, the

The bronze tortoise and crane stand side by side with *jia liang*, a symbolic measurement instrument of stone, in front of the Hall of Supreme Harmony.

largest and tallest of the palace structures that have been preserved to this day anywhere in China. The roof the hall, itself an elaborately decorated structure, is designed in such a way as to indicate the highest status of the hall, and so are the hall's interior decorations. Under the imperial rules, the number of legendary animal figurines on the ridge of a roof was limited to nine for any structure. The Hall of Supreme Harmony, however, is the only exception. Ten figurines are counted on the ridge of its roof - nine animal figurines plus one human figurine. In short, everything was done to make the hall the highest symbol of

the supremacy of the imperial power.

Likewise, the eaves, the doors and windows of the hall were most exquisitely painted. The dragon, seen as the symbol of imperial power and might, is the most frequently used decorative design. Designs of the legendary animal are seen everywhere and on everything - painted on the eaves and carved on the doors, windows and the railings of the platform. Now let ns go in. Dazzling are the six huge columns plated in gold, each with a dragon coiling upward. In the center of the hall, on a platform with seven stairs, there stands the dragon throne. Behind the throne there is a seven-leaf screen, which is painted with dragons dancing in clouds and waves. Believe it or not, as many as more than 12,600 dragons are counted in the hall. A "land of dragons", isn't it?

In front of the Hall of Supreme Harmony, on the marble platform, we find a tortoise and a crane, both of bronze, a stone sundial, and a symbolic measuring instrument called *jia liang*. In ancient times, the tortoise and crane were symbols of long life and happiness. While telling time, the sundial was seen as symbolizing the country's long-term stability. The bronze crane and tortoise on the platform were hollow inside, and were used as sandalwood burners at ceremonies.

The "Three Great Halls" — the Hall of Supreme Harmony, the Hall of
Perfect Harmony and the Hall of Preservation of Harmony.

The three-tier stone platform on which the "Three Great Halls" stand.

Blue is the sky, and bathed in the glory of the bright sun are the red walls, the pure white platform, and the golden roofs of the Hall of Supreme Harmony. Sandalwood smoke are curling upward from the crane, the tortoise and numerous incense burners. Below the platform, the guard of honor stands in full attention, their flags embroidered with dragon designs fluttering in the gentle wind. In full formal court dresses, imperial princes and court ministers gather in front of the hall, holding their breaths in awe. Suddenly, and ever so suddenly, drums and bells begin sounding. Those standing in front of the hall, except the guard of honor, instantly get down on their knees, knowing that the emperor is ascending the dragon throne for the ceremony, their shouting "long live our emperor" resounding in the huge square.

The Hall of Perfect Harmony and the Hall of Preservation of Harmony: The Hall of Perfect Harmony, which lies in between the Hall of Supreme Harmony and the Hall of Preservation of Harmony, is where the emperor readied himself for court meetings or ceremonies. It is therefore smaller than the other two halls and is not as lavishly decorated. The Hall of Preservation of Harmony was the venue of the court examinations, as well as of banquets given by the emperor in honor of the imperial princes. As such, it has a dragon chair in the middle. But it is smaller than the Hall of Supreme Harmony and its interior decorations were not as lavish.

The Hall of Preservation of Harmony has a nine-bay front, suggesting that in status, the structure is lower than the Hall of Supreme Harmony but higher than the Hall of Perfect Harmony that has a five-bay front. The Hall of Perfect Harmony is the smallest of the Three Great Halls. Moreover, it has a square roof. Like its size, the shape of its roof also suggests that it is lower in status than either the Hall of Supreme Harmony or the Hall of Perfect Harmony. The size, shape and interior decoration of each suit perfectly well with its use and status under the imperial hierarchical system. Standing on the same pure white platform, the Three Great Halls, with the smallest in the middle, present a unique atheistic effect that makes the scene awe-inspiring while lively.

The Palace of Heavenly Purity: Descending the platform behind the Hall of Preservation of Harmony, we find one more courtyard in front of us. This is where the frontal part of the Forbidden City and the imperial living quarters join. Lying to the north of the courtyard is the Gate of Heavenly Purity, the main gate of the imperial living quarters. At either side of the gate there is a screen wall with glazed patterns of decoration, the two screen walls arranged in such a way as to form an inverted V. Screen walls - in most cases with carved murals — are often seen in traditional courtyards or at either side of the gate outside. While a decoration, screen walls help protect the privacy of those

living in the courtyards. The screen walls in front of the Gate of Heavenly Purity, however, are just meant to make the courtyard more imposing.

The Palace of Heavenly Purity, the most imposing structure in the imperial living quarters, lies behind the Gate of Heavenly Purity. The palace, in fact a hall, was the bedchamber of the Ming emperors and their crown empresses and, for a time, the imperial bedchamber of the Qing Dynasty. Emperor Yong Zheng, the fifth Emperor of the Qing, did not want to use his dead father's bedchamber and moved to the Hall of Moral Cultivation. After that, the Palace of Heavenly Purity became an imperial office room and a place for imperial audiences

Interior of Palace of Heavenly Purity.

The Palace of Heavenly Purity, the sleeping quarters of the emperor and his queen.

given in honor of foreign diplomats. And as such, it has a dragon throne in the middle.

What is even more important about the Palace of Heavenly Purity is that behind the horizontal board above the dragon throne, the secret decisions in the handwriting of the Qing Dynasty's reigning emperors on appointment of their successors were hidden. Interesting enough, the board is inscribed with the four Chinese characters meaning "upright and honest", even though struggles fought desperately between imperial princes for the dragon throne were common occurrences.

In all dynasties before the Qing, the eldest male child born of the reigning emperor's crown empress was, in most cases, made the crown prince. Even if the crown prince was an idiot, a helpless womanizer or drunkard, he would automatically succeed the throne after his father died. It was Emperor Kang Xi of the Qing Dynasty who broke the tradition. Emperor Kang Xi had 35 sons, who engaged in fierce struggles, overt and covert, for the throne. The fourth son won in the end, and made himself Emperor Yong Zheng after his father died. To prevent a repetition of history, Emperor Yong Zheng decided to keep his decision on appointment of his successor a secret until after he died. He wrote the decision in two copies, one kept by himself and the other, in a locked box hidden behind the horizontal board above the dragon throne in the Hall of Heavenly Purity. After he died, a committee of most senior court ministers opened the box, and announced the dead emperor's decision after verifying both copies as authentic. The new method seemed "honest", but never was it able to achieve the purpose for which it was designed.

The Hall of Earthly Tranquility **and** *the Hall of Union and Peace*: In the Ming Dynasty, the Hall of Earthly Tranquility was where the crown empresses lived. For this reason, it is pretty large, with a nine-bay front. After Emperor Shun Zhi, the third emperor of the Qing Dynasty, settled in the Forbidden City in the mid-1600s, the hall was renovated in following the folk customs of the Manchurians. It was partitioned into two parts, the east part reserved as the imperial nuptial chamber and the west part, as the imperial site for performing rites of shamanism. Though the imperial family of the Qing adopted the Taoist and Buddhist beliefs shortly after their conquest of the Ming, shamanism that characterized their religion continued to be practiced in the Forbidden City. A hog would be slaughtered at such a rite, and its meat boiled and a slice of it given to everyone present on the occasion. Through the large window we can see the stove and the big cauldron used to heat

The three main structures and other buildings in the rear part of the Forbidden City.

water for cleaning the slaughtered hog of its bristles.

The Hall of Union and Peace lies in between the Palace of Heavenly Purity and the Hall of Earthly Tranquility. Originally it had been where the crown empress received good wishes from the emperor's other consorts and princes on her birthday, before it was made the place where the dynasty's 25 state seals were kept. Dragon designs dominate the Three Great Halls in the frontal part of the Forbidden City. In comparison, the Palace of Heavenly Purity, the Hall of Earthly Tranquility and the Hall of Union and Peace in the rear part are decorated with designs of both the dragon and the phoenix. This suggests that the emperor and his crown empress shared these structures, as the phoenix was the symbol of the crown empress.

The three halls in the imperial living quarters stand on the same pure white platform, like the Three Great Halls in the frontal part of the Forbidden City. Moreover, the smallest hall is placed in between the two larger halls, the same way as the Three Great Halls. But these structures are much smaller in size, and the platform is much lower. The Three Great Halls are imposing, designed in such a way as to impress people with the imperial might and power. In comparison, the "three rear halls" look peaceful and even a little homely.

The Imperial Garden: Lying to the north of the Hall of Union and Peace, the Imperial Garden is the last part of the Forbidden City that sits astride the axis of the imperial palace complex. Structures in the garden, however, are not arranged in order of bilateral symmetry, and the main hall, pavilions, corridors, plants and flowers are properly spaced and distributed for a visual impact of natural beauty. In addition to trees and flowers that grow in the relatively cold north, the garden features potted plants and miniature landscapes characteristic of south China, as well as exotic rocks that local government officials sent in as tributes to the emperor.

The Hall of Moral Cultivation: This was the private quarters of Emperor Yong Zheng and the succeeding emperors. Despite that, it does not sit astride the axis of the Forbidden City, as structures of the same status should. Instead, the hall stands in the west part of the

imperial living quarters.

The hall, with a three-bay front, is partitioned into two parts. The frontal part was where individual court ministers were summoned in for questioning by the emperor on state affairs. As such, it has a desk and a chair reserved for his majesty. There are two side chambers in the hall, where the emperor held private discussions with the members of the Council of State — the cabinet or the collective premiership. Pay attention to the curtain hung in front of the side chamber in the east. That curtain is historic. In 1861, Emperor Xian Feng died and his only son, then six years old, ascended the throne as Emperor Tong Zhi. The child emperor's mother, Empress Dowager Ci Xi, became the *de facto* ruler of China. At court meetings in the hall, she would sit behind the screen giving instructions while her son, the child emperor, sat on the dragon chair, supposedly to exercise the imperial power. The

The Gate of Moral Cultivation

Empress, known in the West as "China's fire-spitting dragon lady" for her viciousness and greed for power, reigned supreme until she died in 1908.

The Gate of Divine Prowess: This was the north gate of the Forbidden City. In the Ming Dynasty, it was called the "Xuan Wu Gate", "Xuan Wu" being the name of the God of Water. The name of the gate was changed into "Divine Prowess", reading "shen wu", after Aisinjero Xuan Ye ascended the throne as Emperor Kang Xi. This was done in following the taboo obliging people to avoid the word or phrase that coincided, either in form or pronunciation, with any character in the name of an elder. The Gate of Divine Prowess, so to speak, is in fact a section of the wall surrounding the Forbidden City, with three openings dug through it. A huge hall, not a watchtower, sits atop that section, distinguishing the gate from an ordinary city gate.

We are now outside the Gate of Divine Prowess, having seen those magnificent palace structures and felt the might and power of the monarchs. But, beside what is visible and what can instantly be felt, is there anything else that we should know about the Forbidden City?

The answer is that the Forbidden City, in itself, is the highest embodiment of China's traditional philosophical approach, the concepts of *yin-yang* and *wu xing* that for more than 2,000 years, influenced China and her people in all aspects of life.

Ancient Chinese thinkers held that the universe is formed with two kinds of *qi* called *yin* and *yang*, that exist as a unity of the opposites, and that it is the interplay of these two opposing principles of nature that sparks all changes and movements in the universe. The concept of *yin-yang* was originally used to refer to how the two sides of the same subject faces the sun - the side facing the sun is *yang* and the opposite side, *yin*. As time went by, the *yin-yang* concept became increasingly broad in meaning - *yin* referring to things static, cold, dark, descending or inward while *yang*, to things dynamic, warm, bright, ascending or

The east chamber of the Hall of Moral Cultivation. At court meetings, Empress Dowager Ci Xi would sit on the chair was seated on a dragon chair, supposedly to exercise the imperial powers.

outward. People also made farfetched comparisons between *yin-yang* and natural sciences including mathematics - *yin* referring to round numbers and *yang*, to single numbers. The concept of *wu xing* originally referred to the five elements - the metal, wood, water, fire and earth, which ancient Chinese believed were the basic components of the physical universe. Like the *yin-yang* concept, the concept of *wu xing* was expanded to cover the directions and colors, the "five directions" being east, south, west, north and central, and the "five colors", blue, yellow, red, white and black. The five elements, the five directions and the five colors are often combined according to regular orders. As *yang* refers to the front and man and *yin*, to the back and woman, the frontal part of the Forbidden City was reserved for the handling of state affairs and the rear part, as the imperial living quarters. *Yang* refers to single numbers, hence construction of the Three Great Halls in the frontal part of the Forbidden City. In comparison, the rear part originally had two halls, the Palace of Heavenly Purity and the Hall of Earthly Tranquility, as *yin* refers to round numbers. The Hall of Union and Peace was built decades after the Forbidden City was built.

Yellow is the color of earth, and ancient Chinese believed that life stems from earth. Because of this belief, yellow was regarded as the most important or the most sacred color and, as such, it came to be reserved for the emperor. That explains why bright yellow glazed tiles were used to construct the roofs of those imperial structures. The Hall of Literary Profundity, the emperor's private library, is one of the few exceptions. It has a black roof. Believe it or not, ancient Chinese paired the black color and the water together. As the water overwhelms the fire, the builders thought that the hall, full of books that were easy to burn, would be free from fire by having a black roof. Red was the color of power. In the Ming Dynasty, reports submitted to the emperor must be written on bright red paper. In the Qing Dynasty, documents for circulation by the cabinet on order of the emperors must be copied in red ink. Moreover, red is the auspicious color, the color of happiness. The gates, doors and windows of the imperial structures are all painted bright red, and so are the columns inside them. When overlooking the

Forbidden City from atop the Hill of Prospect facing the Gate of Divine Prowess, we see a set of rainbow hues - golden yellow roofs shining under the clear blue sky, the red walls, the pure white platforms, and, last of all, the ground paved with gray bricks. When the Forbidden City was built, minute attention was paid to colors to make sure that they would be properly used.

Visitors are invariably curious about the stud-studded gates of the Forbidden City. These studs, as a matter of fact, are also symbols of the imperial power and status. In the Ming Dynasty, the gates of the

The Gate of Divine Prowess, the north gate of the Forbidden City, with the Imperial Moat flowing past.

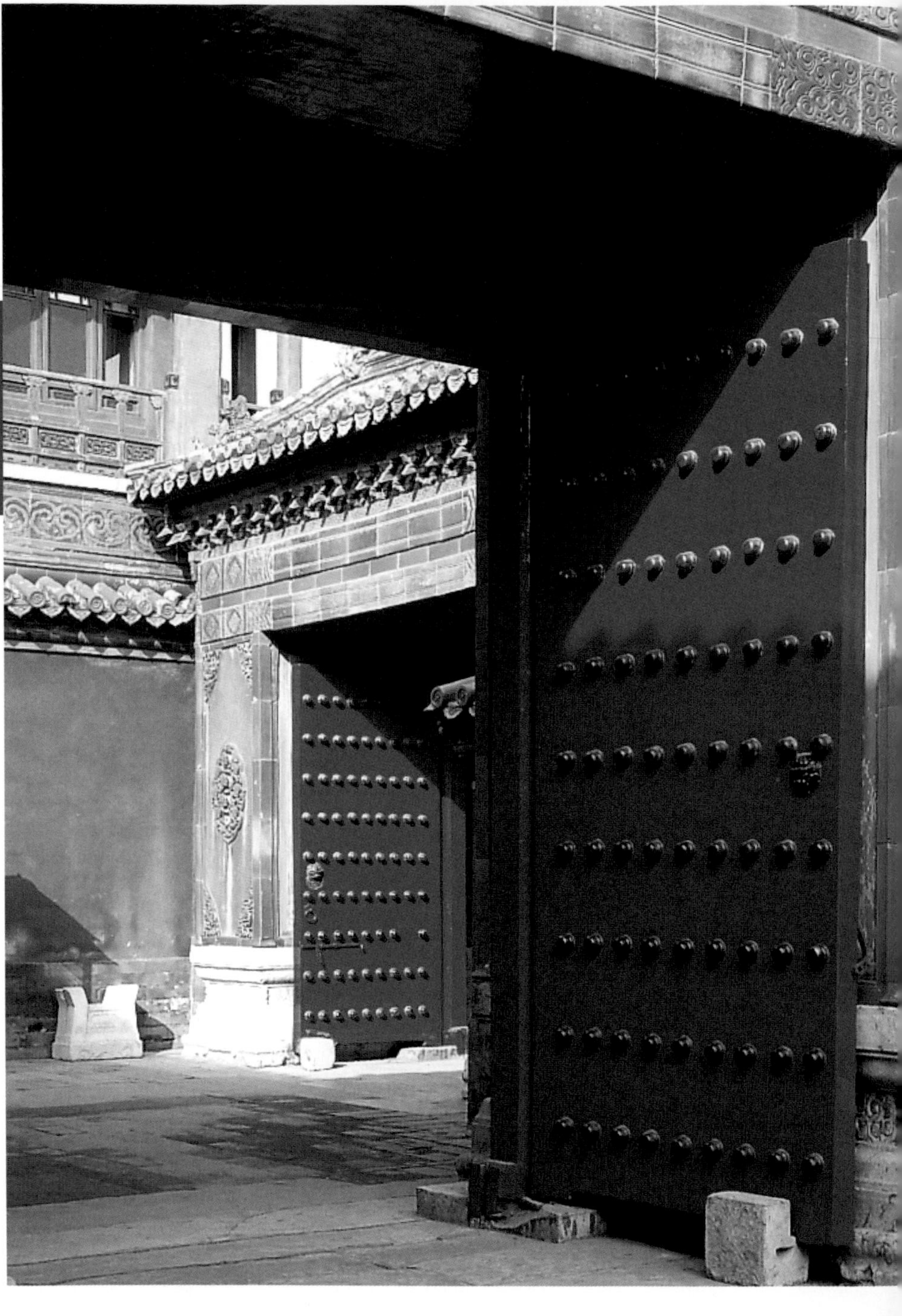

Forbidden City were painted in bright red with 81 golden studs in nine rows. Nine is the greatest of the single numbers, and was therefore reserved for the emperor. Officials, however, must have their gates painted in green or black according to their rankings, with up to 25 studs of bronze or iron. Imperial princes living outside the Forbidden City may have their gates painted in red and the studs in golden yellow. But the number of the studs on a gate must not exceed 49, arranged in seven rows.

While decorative, those small figurines on the roof ridges also indicate the status of their occupiers. These are always in single numbers, with an immortal taking the lead while the others are legendary animals supposedly to guard the structure. Under the patriarchal system, the most important structures in the Forbidden City may have nine figurines on their roof ridges. The only exception is the Hall of Supreme Harmony, on whose roof ridge there are ten.

1. Que is a pavilion-like structure on a raised platform. Such structures are seen in front of palace buildings or imperial mausoleums, one at either side of the front gate.

2. The "Palace City", as the name suggests, is where the emperor and his family lived. Beyond it was the "Imperial City", which was reserved for residences of the nobility and offices of the various ministries. Ordinary people, or commoners, lived in the "Capital City" beyond the "Imperial City".

3. Held in the presence of the emperor, the court examination was the final stage of any sequence of civil service recruitment examinations in feudal China. In fact the emperor personally decided the list of the top three winners in court examination.

Courtyard gates in the Forbidden City.

Altars and Temples

Far back in the prehistory times, the human race was already worshipping their ancestors and what they believed were super-naturals. As human civilization developed, some primitive practices of worshipping continued while some others were lost. In China, worshipping of Heaven, the Earth, the ancestors and the super-naturals had, by the Zhou period about the 11th century BC, culminated into the establishment of a fairly complete system of rites. It continued in the following centuries, in all dynasties, until the country became a republic in 1911.

The main hall in the Temple of Imperial Ancestors.

Altars and temples built in ancient China were meant for practice of rites, or *li zhi*, — a complete system of rituals and ceremonies meant to preserve the established standard for social conduct and human relations. Ancient Chinese attached great importance to the educational role of the rites. To uphold the patriarchal system, stringent rules governing social conduct and etiquette were rigidly enforced, and that was exactly what the rites were meant for. As a rule, the emperor personally presided over the most important official sacrificial ceremonies — those dedicated to Heaven, the Earth and the imperial ancestors — for continuation of the imperial rule and stability of the country. Meanwhile, sacrificial ceremonies were held by all families to beg their ancestors for protection and blessing, mostly on festivals and other important occasions like weddings.

Generally speaking, ceremonies dedicated to the ancestors, gods and dead people of virtue were held in temples or memorial halls. The most typical of these are the Imperial Ancestral Temple in Beijing, the Confucius Temple in the sage's birthplace in Qufu, Shandong Province, as well as family temples found almost everywhere in the country. In comparison, sacrificial ceremonies dedicated to sacred objects in nature were held in the open, before altars built on raised platforms, such as the Altar of Heaven and the Altar of the Earth in Beijing. There are, of course, exceptions. Some sacred objects in nature could be worshipped in temples. One example is the Temple of Mt. Taishan in Shandong.[1]

To sum up, ancient Chinese temples and altars were, without exception, meant to reinforce the rites. These can be divided into three categories: imperial temples and altars for worshipping of Heaven, the Earth, the sun, the moon and the imperial ancestors; commemorative temples for dead people of great virtue; and family temples that can still be found in many places.

Imperial Temples and Altars

The Imperial Ancestral Temple and the Altar of Land and Grain:
As we have already said, the Zhou Dynasty far back in the 11th

Century BC was already practicing a fairly complete system of rites and ceremonies. According to historic records, the ground plan for the dynasty's capital city followed the principle of having the palace complex built in the center, with the temple dedicated to the supreme ruler's ancestors to the left and the altar to the land and grain to the right. This way of planning the most important structures in the capital became a fixed pattern, to be followed by all the Chinese rulers following the Zhou.

Under the hereditary system, the imperial power was passed down within the imperial family, from generation to generation. That explains why Chinese emperors and kings were so keen to ancestral worshipping. Imperial ancestral temples were built in all dynasties, but only one has been preserved to this day. That structure lies to the left of the Forbidden City in the center of Beijing, which served as the Imperial Ancestral Temple for both the Ming and Qing dynasties and now as the Beijing Workers' Cultural Palace. The temple, so to speak, is a neat cluster of one-story buildings in a walled compound. In some ways, it resembles the Forbidden City in ground plan. Like the Forbidden City, the Imperial Ancestral Temple has three palace halls, which sit astride the axis of the north part of the compound. The hall in the front, with an 11-bay front, is where sacrificial ceremonies were held in feudal times and, as such, it stands on a three-layer marble platform while its roof, itself an elaborate structure, is of the highest status. The hall in the center is where the memorial tablets of the dynasty's dead emperors were displayed. The tablets would be moved to the hall in its front when commemorative ceremonies were held. The hall in the rear was used for display of the commemorative tablets of the imperial family's remote ancestors. The three palace halls each have a side hall to either side, round which there are two walls forming two circles, one within the other, with the main gate of the compound in the middle of the south section of the outer wall. Towering cypress trees grow in the courtyard in between the gate and the south section of the inner wall, including many that were planted 500 years ago, making the compound even more solemn and respectful.

The Altar of Land and Grain lies to the right front of the Forbidden City, thus forming a symmetrical pair with the Imperial Ancestral Temple. Agriculture was ancient China's lifeline and, for this reason, land and grain were seen as the symbol of the state. In classical Chinese, the characters 社稷 (land and grain) are synonyms of 江山 (the rivers and mountains) and 天下 (the country). Worshipping of land and grain dates to the times of remote antiquity and, as time went by, people developed the ritual of worshipping them in front of earthen mounds or "altars" as they chose to call them. Before the Ming Dynasty, two earthen mounds symbolizing land and grain separately were built within the same temple. In the Ming Dynasty and the succeeding Qing, however, land and grain came to be worshipped together, hence the Altar of Land and Grain in a compound to the west of the Gate of

Towering cypress trees make the Temple of Imperial Ancestors even more solemn and respectful.

Heavenly Peace.[2] The altar is, in fact, a raised platform one meter high, in the shape of a square with each side measured at 15 meters in length. The surface of the platform is covered with earth of the "five colors", which stand for the Chinese territory in the "five directions" - blue for the east, white for the west, red for the south, and black for the north while yellow, the "imperial color", is in the center. The earth of the "five colors" was from different parts of China, sent to Beijing as a tribute to the emperor. A low wall surrounds the platform, also in the shape of a square, and each side of the wall is decorated with glazed tiles in the color that stands for a specific direction - blue, white, red or black. At a sacrificial ceremony, those present would stand to the north of platform. To shelter the emperor from wind or rain during the ceremony, a hall was built there.

Altars dedicated to Heaven, the Earth, the Sun and the Moon:
As we have said, ancient China was an agricultural country. As agricultural production is often affected by natural adversities, ancient Chinese came to believe that land was essential to their subsistence but

The Altar of the Land and Grain, with earth of five different colors on its surface.

The Altar of Heaven.

harvests were at the mercy of the sun, moon and stars high above, the rain falling from the skies and the wind from all directions. These awed them into worshipping the nature, into begging the nature for blessing before sowing and harvest and into offering sacrifices to Heaven at thanksgiving ceremonies after the annual harvest. Chinese rulers, whether the kings in a divided China under the slavery system or the emperors that reigned supreme over a unified China under feudalism, all took advantage of this superstitious belief to consolidate their political power. They gave themselves the title "Son of Heaven", claiming to rule the country on behalf of Heaven. Heaven worshipping thus became institutionalized, and ceremonies in honor of Heaven were made the most important state ceremonies - even more important than sacrificial ceremonies in honor of the imperial ancestors. All sacrificial ceremonies were banned during the period of mourning after the emperor or the queen mother died. The ceremony in honor of Heaven, however, was the only exception and would be held as planned. Ceremonies in honor of Heaven were a right exclusive to the emperor. Any other person, now matter how high his position was, would be severely punished if he dared to hold such a ceremony. And for the same reason, the altars of Heaven and Earth featured prominently in the capital city of any dynasty.

According to the *yin-yang* philosophy, south is the direction of *yang* and north, the direction of *yin*, and Heaven is referred to as *yang* and the Earth, as *yin*. Besides, the sun rises in the east and the moon, in the west. That explains why the altar of Heaven is always in the south part of the capital city, the altar of the moon, in the north part, the altar of the sun, in the east part, and the altar of the moon, in the west part. Moreover, these altars, as ancient Chinese believed, had to be built on the remote outskirts of the city, far from the city center, so that Heaven, Earth, the sun and the moon would be free from the noise. The Ming and Qing dynasties' altars of Heaven, Earth, the sun and the moon were all built outside the city wall of Beijing. To be more specific, the Temple of Heaven lies beyond the south section of the wall, the Temple of Earth, beyond the north section of the wall, the Altar of the Sun, beyond the east section of the wall, and the Altar of the Moon, beyond the west section of the wall. The Temple of Heaven, however, became a part of the "outer city" in the Ming Dynasty as a result of the building of an outer wall.[3]

The Temple of Heaven, with the Altar of Heaven, the Imperial Vault of Heaven and the Hall of Prayer for Good Harvest on a straight line from south to north.

The caisson in the Imperial Vault of Heaven, which is recognized as a best example of this unique type of ceilings in traditional-style buildings.

The Temple of Heaven was built in 1420, the year when construction of the Forbidden City was completed. Some structures in the temple were renovated and a few more structures were built in the Qing Dynasty, but the ground plan and the most important structures remained intact. The temple occupies an area of 2.78 million square metes, four times as large as the Forbidden City. But buildings there are relatively few and large tracts of the area are covered with trees.

Here we are at the main gate of the temple at the west section of the wall that surrounds the complex. After we step in, we find ourselves on a long, straight road ahead of us. At the south side of the west section of the road there stands the Hall of Abstinence, where the emperor stayed for fasting before sacrificial ceremonies in honor of Heaven. Three days before such a ceremony, the emperor would move to the Hall of Abstinence. To "purify" his body and soul out of respect for Heaven, he would, during these three days, refrain from drinking wine, eating meat and strong smelling foods like leeks and garlic, and having carnal pleasure.

The main structures in the Temple of Heaven, however, are the Altar of Heaven, the Imperial Vault of Heaven and the Hall of Prayer for Good Harvest, which stand from south to north, at east side of the

Imperial Vault of Heaven.

road.

The Altar of Heaven, as the name suggests, was the venue of sacrificial ceremonies dedicated to Heaven. It is a three-layer round mound, each layer surrounded by a concentric railing of pure white marble. Two walls surround the platform, one enclosed within the other. The inner wall is round and the outer wall forms a square. Beyond the outer wall there is a forest of towering cypress tress, which helps create an atmosphere of solemnity and respect. The Heaven-worshipping ceremony was held before dawn on the day of the Winter Solstice every year. The emperor would ascend the mound, amid the sound of music played by the imperial orchestra. High on the poles in front of the mound hung bright red lanterns. Smoke of sandalwood kept curling up from a dozen burners at the southeast side of the mound. Everything was designed to add mystery to the occasion. At the end of the ceremony, sacrificial articles in paper and silk were burned in the same burners, the emperor and his subjects believing that the curling smoke would carry these to Heaven.

The Imperial Vault of Heaven to the north of the Altar of Heaven was where the memorial tablet of Heaven was displayed. It is a round one-story structure, with a smaller hall at either side. A stone wall in a perfect circle surrounds the Imperial Vault of Heaven. What is peculiar about the wall is that the stones are so finely polished that anything said at one side of it, even in a low voice, can be picked up at the other side. The acoustic effect of this "Echo Wall", as it is called, was however not deliberately designed.

Stepping out of the north gate of the Imperial Vault of Heaven, we see, ahead of us, a broad, straight avenue. Large tracts of ever-green trees - pines and cypresses, etc. - flank the avenue, which is 360 meters long and 30 meters wide and is raised four meters above the ground. Taking a stroll along the avenue with so broad a vision under the blue sky, we feel as if we were melting into a vast sea of blue and green, into the embrace of Heaven that overlooks the world from high up in the universe. The kind of artistic conception we are getting hold of is exactly what the designers and builders of the Temple of Heaven wanted to create, an artistic conception commensurate with the full solemnity and respect that characterized the imperial ceremonies.

At the end of the Avenue, we find one more group of structures, which is nonetheless meant for prayer for good crop years. The main structure is the Hall of Prayer for Good Harvest, a cone-shaped structure that features an elaborate roof with three eaves at different heights. Like other imperial structures of major importance, it stands on a pure white marble platform, and is flanked by side halls and surrounded by

The avenue in front of the Hall of Prayer for Good Harvest.

walls.

The Temple of Heaven, as we can see now, is designed to serve two functions, Heaven worshipping and prayer for good harvests. But how the ancient Chinese architects fulfilled the demanding task of arranging the different structures in such a way as to suit the dual purpose?

Perfect use of symbolism is the answer.

Ancient Chinese saw the universe or Heaven as an immeasurably large vault hanging above the ground, and the land as a neat square. That is why things symbolizing Heaven are always in the shapes of circles or cylinders and things denoting land, in the shape of squares. The three main structures in the Temple of Heaven, the Altar of Heaven, the Imperial Vault of Heaven and the Hall of Prayer for Harvest, are all conical in shape. The walls surrounding them, however, form three neat squares.

The numbers are also symbolic. As ancient Chinese saw it, Heaven and the emperor should be referred to *yang*. So should be single numbers. Nine is the biggest single number. As such, nine and numbers multiplied by nine are most frequently used in structures for exclusive use by the emperor including, of course, those in the Temple of Heaven. Take, for example, the Altar of Heaven or the "Circular Mound" as it is

A bird's-eye-view of the Hall of Prayer for Good Harvest.

The Hall of Prayer for Good Harvest.

called for convenience. The top of the mound is covered with stone slabs. The slab in the center is round. Round the center there are nine enclosures, one within another. The innermost enclosure is formed with nine stone slabs, the second enclosure, with 18, the third, with 27, the fourth, with 36, and in the outermost enclosure, 81 stone slabs are counted. The railings on the marble platforms are also in numbers multiplied by nine - those of the top layer numbering 36, those in the middle, 72, and those in the bottom, 108. The platforms each have a terraced stairs with nine steps.

The Hall of Prayer for Harvest, however, is different, involving numbers that are associated, one way or another, with agricultural production. The pillars of the hall form three circles, which support the three-eave roof of the structure. The outermost circle consists of 12 pillars supporting the outermost eave, which symbolize the 12 two-hour periods into which the day is traditionally divided. The circle in the middle also consists of 12 pillars, which symbolize the 12 months of the year. The 24 pillars symbolize the 24 periods, approximately 15 days each, into which the lunar year is divided. The inner most four pillars that support the top layer of the roof denote the four seasons of

A temple dedicated to Mt. Hengshan, one of the five sacred mountains. Mt. Hengshan is in Shanxi Province, but the temple is in Quyang County of the neighboring Hebei Province.

the year.

The land is yellow, and the sky is blue. This visual impression generated by nature made the yellow color symbolic of the land and the blue color, of Heaven. That explains why blue is the dominant color of the Temple of Heaven. Tiles glazed in blue are used to decorate the top of the walls that surrounds the Altar of Heaven and the Round Mound, and so are the walls that surround the courtyards. The Roof of the Hall of Prayer for Harvest is covered with blue glazed tiles, and so are the roofs of the side halls. The blue color matches perfectly with the pure white marble platforms and the evergreen trees around, creating an atmosphere strong enough to keep people in awe of Heaven.

The altars dedicated to the land, sun and moon lie beyond old Beijing's outer city. The three altars, all with facilities for preparing sacrificial food and storehouses of sacrificial utensils, are smaller than the Altar of Heaven dedicated to the supreme ruler of the universe. Like the Altar of Heaven, however, the structures are largely symbolic.

The Altar of Land, for example, is in the north suburbs of Beijing because north is referred to as *yin*, relative to south which is referred to as *yang*. Round numbers are referred to as *yin*, and that is why the altar is a two-layer mound with four straight sides and has four terraced stairs with eight steps each.

Famous rivers and mountains were also worshipped in ancient China. The Five Sacred Mountains all have magnificent temples dedicated to their respective gods. Mt. Taishan in Shandong Province, the most important of the five mountains, has a temple as magnificent as a palace complex on its south slope. Newly enthroned emperors would hold elaborate ceremonies on Mt. Taishan to beg Heaven and land for blessing. The ceremony dedicated to Heaven was always held on the top of Mt. Taishan, and the ceremony dedicated to land, at its foot.

Commemorative Structures

With a brilliant history and culture, ancient Chinese produced numerous outstanding people — scholars noted for their contribution to the development of the Chinese civilization, soldiers who died in wars in defense of the country, and officials who defied death to uphold justice in defiance of imperial orders. Many of them were accorded posthumous honors, hence those commemorative structures we can still see everywhere.

The Confucius temples: Confucius (551 BC - 479 BC), a thinker, educator and philosopher, was the founder of Confucianism, a philosophical school to become China's dominating ideology for well over 2,000 years from around the beginning of the Christian era to the early 20th century. He had the honorific title "sage" in all feudal dynasties, and temples dedicated to him were built in all cities and towns.

The largest and most magnificent Confucius temple, however, is in Qufu, Shandong Province, the sage's birthplace. The Confucius Temple of Qufu was originally the sage's residence, which underwent expansion under all dynasties until it became such as to match the Forbidden City in splendor.

The temple, so to speak, occupies an area of 32,700 square meters — measured at 650 meters from north to south — in which there are structures with a total of 460 rooms. It consists of two parts. The part in the front features three stone archways and five gates. Of the four great halls in the rear part, the largest and most important is the Hall of Great Literary Attainment, where a portrait of Confucius is displayed for worshipping. The Hall of Great Literary Attainment has a roof as large and elaborate as the roof of the Hall of Preservation of Harmony, the second largest of the Three Great Halls in the Forbidden City. Ten huge columns with coiling dragons in relief support the eave of the hall. The Hall of Great Literary Attainment stands on a two-layer stone platform with a large front, where ceremonies were held in commemoration of Confucius. Xingtan, or the Apricot Platform in front of the hall, is the site where Confucius taught his disciples. Emperors of all dynasties sent official delegations to pay homage to the sage at the temple, and many came in person. Emperor Yong Zheng of the Qing Dynasty, who reigned from 1723 to 1735, went so far as to decree use of bright yellow glazed tiles — reserved for imperial structures — on structures in the Confucius Temple. Though smaller in size, Confucius temples elsewhere are similar to that in Qufu in ground plan, with, for example, halls and gates named as "great literary attainment".

The Hall of Great Literary Attainment, the Confucius Temple of Qufu.

Some Confucius temples, *alias* "literary temples", were used as government-run schools as well.

Temples of the military: In the third century AD, China came to be divided into three kingdoms, the kingdoms of Wei, Shu and Wu, amid incessant wars and internal conflicts as the Han Dynasty was collapsing. Liu Bei, emperor of the Shu in southwest China, had two great soldiers, Guan Yu and Zhang Fei, as his sworn brothers, and Zhu'ge Liang , a great statesman and strategist, as his prime minister and military advisor. Guan Yu and Zhang Fei has been respected for bravery and gallantry ever

Temple dedicated to Zhang Fei, Yunyang County, Sichuan Province.

since the Three Kingdoms Period, and Zhu'ge Liang, as the very personification of wisdom, resourcefulness and loyalty. Stories about the four heroes of the Shu spread all over China, culminating in the classical novel *Romance of the Three Kingdoms* by Luo Guanzhong of the late Ming Dynasty. The novel, still popular today, has made them known to virtually every Chinese. The four heroes personified the moral principles of Confucianism on benevolence, justice, propriety, wisdom and honesty, prompting construction of memorial temples in their honor everywhere, in Sichuan, their power base, in particular. They were so intimate to one another that more often than not, they are worshipped together, as a collective. In the Zhu'ge Liang Memorial Temple in Chengdu, capital of what is now Sichuan Province, statues of Liu Bei

Temple dedicated to Li Bing and his son, who have been worshipped for well over 2,000 years for construction of the Dujiangyan Weirs.

and Zhang Fei are displayed as well. Likewise, a temple in Zizhong, Sichuan, features the three sworn brothers, Liu Bei, Guan Yu and Zhang Fei, even though it is called the Guan Yu Memorial Temple. For his loyalty and virtue, Guan Yu, in particular, became a divine figure — the "God of War". Temples dedicated to Guan Yuan are, therefore, also referred to as "military temples". In many Chinese cities, "military temples" are found alongside Confucius temples, *alias* "literary temples".

Memorial temples dedicated to Bao Zheng: Bao Zheng, or "Lord Bao the Clear Sky" as he has been referred to, has been no less popular than the four heroes of the Shu Kingdom, hence the numerous temples in his memory. The most famous of the Bao Zheng temples is in his birthplace, Hefei City of Anhui Province. This Song Dynasty (960-1127) official has been held as the highest model of official honesty, fairness, virtue and impartiality, and stories of how he defied the powerful, including even the emperor, to protect the oppressed and humiliated are told in numerous traditional operas and literary works.

The Dujiangyan Weirs, a water control project on a tributary of the Yangtze River, was built in the fourth century BC under the guidance of Li Bing, a local official, and his son. The project is still being used, to the benefit of tens of millions in the Chengdu Plain, the breadbasket of southwest China. Ever since they died, the father and son have been worshipped at a temple in Guanxian County, the site of a bifurcation structure to prevent flooding by the Minjiang River of the Chengdu

Du Fu (712-770), a poet of the Tang Dynasty, has always been remembered as the "sage of Chinese poetry". The Du Fu Cottage in Chengdu was built in his honor.

Plain. There are also structures in commemoration of ancient Chinese writers, poets, scholars and other men and women with outstanding literary achievements. For literary achievements and sympathy towards the laboring people, Du Fu (712-770), a poet of the Tang Dynasty, has always been remembered as the "sage of Chinese poetry". The Du Fu Cottage in Chengdu was built in his honor.

What are the characteristics of these commemorative structures left over from ancient times? In the first place, they are invariably in the places where the persons were born, lived or worked for a period or all their lives. As a matter of fact, some had been the persons' residences that were expanded after they died. That explains why such structures are free in architectural style and ground plan, in many ways resembling local dwellings. The Zhang Fei Temple in Yunyang County, Sichuan Province, stands on the south bank of the Yangtze River, facing the town on the opposite bank where the county government is seated. The temple's main halls and subsidiary structures are distributed evenly on the slope of a hill, and most of them have flying eaves and roofs of

The structure serves as a temple dedicated to Zhuge Liang and, at the same time, the ancestral temple of the Zhuge clan in Lanxi County, Zhejiang Province.

The ancestral temple of the Jin clan in a village in Wuyuan County, Jiangxi Province.

glazed tiles. The Li Bing and Son Temple overlooks the Minjiang River from atop a hill. The entrance is at the foot of the hill, while the main hall, the Li Bing Hall, stands atop the hill. The walled compound has four gates facing different directions. Enclosed in the compound is a cluster of structures — halls, archways, pavilions, towers and a theater on one section of the wall with a gate in its lower part. From the entrance to the main hall we walk up the hill, enjoying the magnificent scenery down the hill at different heights and from different angles.

Temples of this kind are dedicated to people noted for the historic contributions they made to the development of the Chinese nation or the exemplary role they played in the process. Over the centuries these people have always commanded the respect of the people, prompting people to build temples in their honor so that the kind of spirit or moral standards they represented could be passed down from generation to generation. In a nutshell, temples built by people spontaneously played the same role of mass education as the Confucius temples built by the government. The Lord Bao Temple in Hebei constitutes a sharp contrast to the extravagantly decorated Confucius temples. It is a simple

The theater in an ancestral temple, Zhejiang Province.

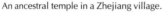

An ancestral temple in a Zhejiang village.　　Brick relieves flank the gate of the Chens' ancestral Temple in Guangzhou.

courtyard, with a hall in which a statue of the Song Dynasty official is displayed for worshipping and his instructions to his family are written on one of the walls. The courtyard, in itself, embodies the kind of honesty and cleanness "Lord Bao, the Clean Sky" upheld all his life.

Family and Clan Temples

Ancient Chinese were deeply family-bound. More often than not, people of the same family line live in the same village. United by blood relations, a family or clan in ancient China often formed a clan-based autonomous body. The head of the body, normally a male elder who commanded high respect of the clan, supervised over the handling of important affairs related to the clan. This autonomous body was well organized, preserved by a set of patriarchal rules and regulations that observed a stringent order of the senior and the junior, those born of legal wives and those born of concubines, and those who were masters and those who were servants. This patriarchal system was, in fact, the foundation of China's feudal government, an instrument by means of which government decisions on political and public affairs were executed. The family or clan saw to it that members pay taxes in time. It was also responsible for mediating settlement of disputes, "enlightening" clan members through education, and organizing sacrificial activities in honor of gods and ancestors.

Each clan had an ancestral hall or temple. While the venue of sacrificial activities in honor of the clan's ancestors, the ancestral hall or temple was the clan's meeting place. It became clan's courtroom where disputes were settled and clan members having broken clan rules punished. Many ancestral temples had theaters, schools and public granary where relief grain was stored. Ancestral temples were often larger in size and better in construction quality than residential buildings of the average level.

In most cases, an ancestral temple consists of several halls in a courtyard, but there are ancestral temples with just one hall each. Ancestral temples of large clans are enclosed in compounds that consist of several courtyards, each courtyard featuring a main hall with side halls on either side. The more powerful and prosperous a clan was, the larger and more magnificent would be its ancestral temple. Now wonder. The temple, after all, was the symbol of the past glory of the clan and its present prosperity and influence.

Again let's say something more about Zhu'ge Liang. Some of his descendents left Sichuan in China's deep southwest for official posts at Lanxi, Zhejiang Province, on the east China coast, where they eventually settled. This branch of the Zhu'ge family grew in size with each passing generation, and eventually built a town named after Zhu'ge. The Zhu'ge Town, so to speak, gathers the largest number of Zhu'ge Liang's descendents. Besides, it is reputed for the Temple of the Prime Minister, which serves as the memorial temple in honor of Zhu'ge Liang and the ancestral temple of the Zhu'ge clan. The temple lies at the entrance of the town, in front of a pond. Here we are in the temple, a compound surrounded on three sides by verandas. What is

The Chens' ancestral Temple in Guangzhou.

most eye-catching, however, is the hall in the middle with a high roof, which is open on the four sides like a pavilion. Stepping into the hall, a careful observer won't miss those exquisitely carved beams and pillars. Behind the hall, the clan's memorial hall of Zhu'ge Liang stands on a raised platform, which also serves as the clan's ancestral hall. On the eve of the Spring Festival, all members of the clan will gather at the temple for a ceremony to offer sacrifices to their common ancestor, Zhu'ge Liang. A clan meeting will follow, at which men and women at 70 or older are wined and dined while steamed bread are given to younger persons. The ritual is meant to remind clan members of the need to always keep in mind their ancestors' blessings.

If palace structures can be taken as representing the highest architectural achievements made in a given dynasty, then it will be safe to say that ancestral temples crystallize the highest architectural achievements by local architects. A good example is the Chens' Ancestral Temple in Guangzhou City, capital of the coastal Guangdong Province, whose construction began in 1890 and was completed in 1894. This is the ancestral temple for all natives of Guangdong whose family name is Chen, hence its size — 19 structures in six courtyards that are arranged in three neat rows, with a combined construction space of more than 8,000 square meters. A memorial tablet dedicated to the common ancestors of the Chens is worshipped in the largest hall in the rear part of the compound. This and the largest hall in the frontal part of the compound are also meeting places. The smaller halls on either side of the largest halls are classrooms of a clan school. Because of that, the Chens' Ancestral Temple is also known as the Chens' Academy of Learning. Beside its size, the Chens' Ancestral Temple or the Chen's Academy of Learning is reputed for exquisite carvings on its stone columns and pillars, wooden beams, bricks and the lime surfaces of some structural parts. It is, in fact, a museum of traditional Chinese carvings. Like the temple itself, the carvings are material testimony to the influence and glamour of the Chen clan and respect of clan members for their common ancestors.

1. Mt. Taishan, or the "East Mountain", tops on the list of the "five sacred mountains" in China. Throughout the feudal times, it received numerous horrific titles.

2. The compound now serves as the Zhongshan Park.

3. In 1533, work began to build one more wall - the outer wall — round the capital city to strengthen Beijing's defense. The project came to a halt after construction was completed on the south section of the wall. So the capital city came to be known as the "inner city", and the part to the south of the capital city, as the "outer city".

Tombs and Mausoleums

Ancient Chinese were superstitious, believing that death just meant the extinction of the body and, after a person died, the person's soul would continue to exist in the nether world, hence the great importance they attached to funerals. As the country is vast in area and has diverse ethnic groups, traditional funerals vary in style form from region to region and from ethnic group to ethnic group. People of the Han majority used to bury the dead in the ground.[1] Chinese Moslems have always followed Islamic traditions in arranging funerals. In northwest China, dead Moslems are wrapped in white cloth for burial and have a mosque-like structure built on where they are buried. Celestial burials are popular among Tibetans in the Tibet Autonomous Region, by which dead bodies are cut into pieces and every bit of the flesh and bones is fed to birds of

Tombs in Islamic style, Turpan Depression, Xinjiang.

prey.

Ancestral worshipping dates back to prehistory times. In China's feudal times that lasted for more than 2,000 years, it underwent changes under the influence of Confucianism, culminating in the establishment of a complete set of rituals that were rigidly enforced throughout the centuries. Tombs and mausoleums became the second most important sites for ancestral worshipping, following ancestral temples. Confucianism stresses the importance of filial piety, regarding it as the foundation of the country's patriarchal system based on blood relations. So long as a person devotedly performs his or her filial duties to the family elders, Confucianism holds, it would be unlikely for the person to defy his or her superiors and neither will the person do anything rebellious. Confucianism goes so far as to oblige people to continue performing filial duties even to their dead elders. In ancient times, people regularly visited graves of their elders to offer sacrifices and "report" what was happening in the family, believing that their elders "living" in the neither words would receive the sacrifices and hear what they said.[2] Before a man left home for travel, he would visit the grave of his parents, "informing" them of his plans and begging them for blessing. When he returned, he would visit the grave again, "telling" them that he had been safe and sound. According to Confucianism, a proper funeral should be arranged immediately after a person dies, so that the person's soul will be in peace. Graves, therefore, were seen as "residences" of the dead, as important as the real residences occupied by the dead when they were alive.

Ordinary people, who could hardly make ends meet, certainly found it difficult to spend too much on funerals and graves. Aristocrats, ranking officials and rich landlords and merchants, however, never hesitated to spend lavishly on funerals. The most extravagant tombs always belonged to emperors. Believe it or not, Chinese emperors would order their own tombs built almost immediately after they were enthroned. They would demand that the tombs be as extravagant as the palaces they were occupying, so that in the nether world, they would be able to enjoy the same kind of life as they were leading. Never would they care about the construction cost.

Under patriarchal rules, tombs and mausoleums, along with their superstructures, had to vary in size and grandeur, depending on the social status of their occupiers, and the principle was applicable to the number of burial objects. Imperial tombs are of the greatest archeological value because they are the largest and most imposing.

Those imperial tombs that have survived the times invariably consist of two parts, the "underground palaces" and the superstructures. The underground palaces, mostly built with stone and bricks, are where the coffins of the dead emperors are kept, along with elaborate arrays of burial objects. The structures on the ground are often enclosed in a large compound, where sacrificial ceremonies were held in honor of the dead emperors. On either side of the long, straight "divine boulevard" in front of the compound there stands a neat queue of stone statues of court ministers, generals and animals — real or legendary — that serve as the dead emperor's guard of honor. A dead emperor's tomb is, in fact, a neat group of imperial structures. In addition to the divine boulevard, we find, in and outside the compound, a whole range of gates, archways and halls and a pavilion that shelters a huge stone tablet dedicated to the memory of the dead emperor. The entire tomb areas is covered with green with pine and cypress trees, symbols of long life.

Imperial Tombs of the Qin and Han Dynasties

Right after he unified China in 221 BC, Emperor Shi Huang of the Qin Dynasty ordered construction, simultaneously, of an imperial palace and a tomb for himself. According to historic records, the underground part of the tomb resembles the real world in minute details while a treasure house of pearls and precious stones. A large number of stone statues of court ministers and generals accompany the dead emperor in the tomb chambers. Fish oil lamps light the chambers, and the ceiling of the main chamber is engraved with a chart of the celestial body while the floors feature "rivers" — in fact ditches filled with mercury. The gate is fitted with a complicated mechanical device by means of

A part of the underground army supposedly to guard the tomb of Emperor Shi Huang of the Qin Dynasty.

which arrows are released the moment a tomb robber breaks in.

The tomb has never been opened. The part of the tomb on the ground, however, is still there, a pyramid-like earthen mound 42 meters high, with a flat top and four sides measured at 350 meters each. The mound is enclosed in two rectangular walls, one within the other, the inner wall being 2,500 meters in circumference and the outer wall, 6,500 meters. Through excavation of the tomb site since the 1980s, archeologists have unearthed thousands of life-size terracotta soldiers and battle steeds, as well as bronze chariots. The underground "army", supposedly to guard the tomb, consists of foot soldiers, archers, crossbow men and cavalrymen, all "battle-ready" but with different facial expressions. Each human figure consists of seven parts — the head, hands, body, legs, etc., which were produced separately, through an elaborate process of clay sculpturing, firing, coloring and assemble.

The part of the terracotta "army" is already great enough to constitute a cultural wonder of global dimension even though only a few of the pits for burial objects have been excavated. Moreover, these are outside the tomb, in the area for burial objects. We are justified to imagine that if opened, the tomb, built by some 700,000 workmen, will turn out to be the world's greatest museum of cultural wonders.

The succeeding Han Dynasty attached no small an importance to building of tombs and mausoleums, which are, nonetheless, guarded by statues of real and legendary animals if the occupiers were important enough. One example is the tomb of Huo Qubing, a brilliant soldier under Emperor Wu Di (156-87 BC) of the Han Dynasty. At 18, Huo already distinguished himself for bravery in battles in defense of the country's northern borders. After he tied at 24, the emperor, in recognition of his military exploits, ordered 14 stone statues to be placed in front of his tomb, including oxen, horses, elephants, tigers, pigs, fish, plus a human figure holding a bear in his arms. These statues are superb artworks, succinct in style while beautifully shaped.

In front of some Han tombs, stone structures known as *que* can still

be seen. A *que* is a stone watchtower with two columns supporting a roof resembling a real roof of timber. The dynasty's wooden structures have all perished, hence the importance of those stone structures to our study of China's architectural art in the dynasty that ruled some 2,000 years ago. Two such towers are

Restored sketch of a *que* in front of a Han Dynasty tomb in Ya'an, Sichuan Province. A *que* is a stone watchtower with two columns supporting a roof resembling a real roof of timber.

The tomb shared by Emperor Gao Zong of the Tang Dynasty and his crown empress Wu Zetian. The hill in the background is Mt. Liangshan where the couple was buried inside a tunnel.

placed in front of the tomb, at the entrance of the tomb area. Behind the watchtowers are stone statues standing on both sides of the divine boulevard.

None of the known imperial tombs of the Han Dynasty has been excavated, but those tombs belonging to imperial princes that have been opened may serve to show us how the inside of an imperial tomb looks like. The burial chamber is rectangular, and a large tomb usually has several inter-connected chambers with walls and floors built with bricks or polished stone. Tombs of the early Han period have ceilings of large bricks or stone slabs. Tombs of the late Han period, however, feature vaults built with layers upon layers of bricks. Relieves are often done on stones and bricks in Han tombs. Some of the relieves picture animals and plants by employing simple, crude lines. There are also relieves painstakingly done to depict the life of the tombs' occupiers in the real world — banqueting, hunting, travels, collecting rent, etc. Sowing, harvesting, salt producing etc. are also themes of Han Dynasty relieves on bricks and stone. While succinct in style, the images are highly impressive. Horses, for example, can be pictured as standing,

A 13th century tomb in Houma, Shanxi Province. The brick relieves depict the life of its occupier, Dong Ming.

neighing or galloping through use of a few simple lines. While highly valued art objects, the stone and brick relieves left over from the Han Dynasty provide ample material evidence to study of the ancient Chinese people and society.

Imperial Tombs of the Tang and Song Dynasties

Feudalism experienced its heyday during the Tang Dynasty (618-907). As the country was gaining strength and prosperity, the first few Tang emperors became increasingly keen to the magnificence of the tombs they were to occupy after death while sparing no effort to expand the imperial complex they were living in. Emperor Taizong, the second Tang emperor who reigned supreme from 626 to 649, was no longer satisfied with the traditional practice of building a mound with earth from digging of the burial pits to indicate where a dead person was buried. He was the first to have a tunnel dug into an imposing hill for use as his tomb. The tomb shared by Emperor Gao Zong and his crown empress Wu Zetian[3] is the best representative of the dynasty's imperial tombs. The tomb is on Mt. Liangshan in Qianxian County under the jurisdiction of Xi'an City, whose peak, rising 1,047 meters above sea level, overlooks two smaller hills to its south. The tomb is a tunnel dug into Mt. Liangshan, on its north slope, halfway from the peak. More than 100 stone statues stand at both sides of the divine boulevard at the foot of Mt. Liangshan in the south. The statues, of not only Chinese civil and military officials but also rulers of China's neighboring countries, testify to the kind of overweening characteristic of Chinese monarchs who regarded their empire as the center of the world and themselves as the rulers of "all land within the four seas".

The Song Dynasty (960-1279), however, was much weaker than the Tang, its northern borders constantly falling prey to invasion and harassment by ethnic minority tribes. Imperial tombs of the dynasty are, therefore, significantly smaller. The Song Dynasty, in fact, banned construction of tombs for emperors and crown empresses before they died. It is only after an emperor died would a tomb be built for him, and the burial must take place in no more than seven months from the day of the emperor's death. That explains why the dynasty's imperial tombs are not only small in size but also duplicated in design. All the nine emperors of the North Song Dynasty (960-1127) were buried in Gongxian County, Henan Province. Each tomb is an earthen mound in a walled compound with a watchtower at each corner, and in front of the compound there is the divine boulevard flanked by stone statues.

A Song Dynasty imperial tomb in Gongxian County, Henan Province. The burial chamber is beneath the earthen mound, with the "divine boulevard" still visible.

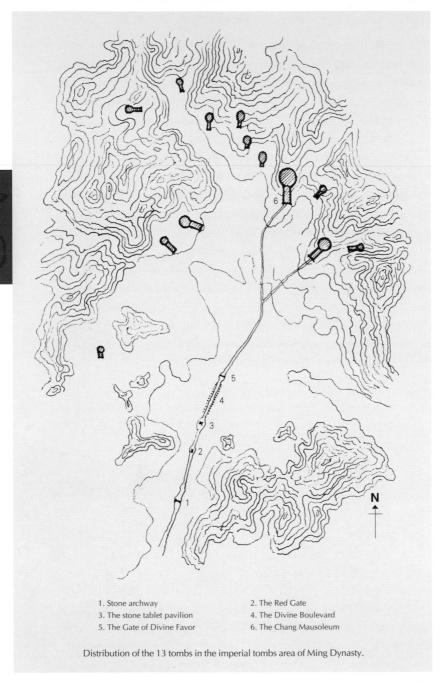

1. Stone archway
2. The Red Gate
3. The stone tablet pavilion
4. The Divine Boulevard
5. The Gate of Divine Favor
6. The Chang Mausoleum

Distribution of the 13 tombs in the imperial tombs area of Ming Dynasty.

Though not as imposing and magnificent as imperial tombs of the Han and Tang dynasties, the nine tombs of the Song are within walking distance from one another. The way of having the emperors buried in the same place was to continue into the Ming and Song dynasties.

None of the Song Dynasty's imperial tombs have been opened. In some north China provinces like Henan, Hebei and Shanxi, Song tombs belonging to rich merchants or government officials have been excavated. The burial chambers, mostly stone and brick structures, are pretty small, some only about two square meters large, but the murals and relieves depicting the tombs' occupiers in the real world are invaluable. The burial chamber of one Song Dynasty tomb features relieves of the occupier's house on three sides of the brick wall — a cluster of one-story buildings with windows and doors to allow in sufficient sunshine and fresh air. On the south side of the wall, the tomb's occupier and his wife are depicted as sitting at the either side of a table laden with food and flowers, watching a theatrical performance on the stage in the opposite. The lines are so fine and exquisite that the facial expressions of the figures are clearly discernible, in a style of realism that characterized the architectural art of tombs and mausoleums built in the Song Dynasty.

Imperial Tombs of the Ming Dynasty

In 1368, Zhu Yuanzhang,[4] leader of the most powerful rebel army in peasant uprisings against the Yuan Dynasty, topped the Mongol regime and made himself Emperor Tai Zu of the Ming. In his opinion, the Ming Dynasty (1368-1644) ushered in the rebirth of China's ethnic Han majority group who had been ruled for nearly a century by the Mongols, an ethnic minority group. The new emperor was, therefore, resolved to carry forward the feudal traditions initiated by Confucius and developed by the Han rulers of the dynasties before the Ming. And to this end, he spared no effort to promote Confucianism and restore those ceremonial forms that characterized the patriarchal system. Shortly after it came into being, the Ming Dynasty promulgated a set of stringent rules concerning funerals for officials of different rankings, banned

The Divine Boulevard of Emperor Taizu, the Ming Dynasty.

cremation and water burials, and made practice by Han people of the Mongol burial customs a crime punishable under the Imperial Criminal Code.[5] Zhu Yuangzhang was buried in Nanjing, the "south capital", where he set up the Ming Dynasty. His tomb, known as the Xiaoling Mausoleum of the Ming Dynasty, features a divine boulevard with stone statues at both sides of it, which leads to the Hall of Divine Favor, the venue of sacrificial ceremonies in honor of the dead emperor. Behind the Hall of Divine Favor there stands a pavilion-like watchtower, which shades a large stone tablet dedicated to the dead emperor. The dead emperor is buried behind the watchtower, the part of the tomb on the ground forming a large round earthen mound named as the "Sacred City". The ground plan for the tomb of the Ming Dynasty's founding emperor was to be followed in construction of the tombs for all succeeding emperors of the dynasty.

In 1420, the national capital was officially moved to Beijing on order of the third Ming emperor, Zhu Di. Construction of the Forbidden City, however, began far back in 1407, which was to proceed along with work in search of a place with a geomantic quality good enough for imperial tombs. The site was chosen finally, at Mt. Heavenly Longevity, a chain of rolling hills in Changping on the north outskirts of Beijing that encircles a vast expanse of flatland — a basin, in fact — on three sides. Zhu Di, or Emperor Yong Le as he chose to title himself, had his own tomb built on the north fringe of the basin, facing south at the foot of Mt. Heavenly Longevity. The 12 emperors that followed him had their tombs built on the east fringe of the basin or the west, supposedly to accompany their common ancestor in the heaven. Though independent of one another, the 13 Ming Tombs, as they were

The Chang Mausoleum

collectively referred to, were however built under a general construction plan, have a common gate and share the Divine Boulevard.

The 13 Ming Tombs occupy an area of 40 square kilometers. The gate of on the south end of the Divine Boulevard extending to the north. Looking around, we find ourselves being honored by the "imperial guard of honor" standing on either side — stone statues of six animals in 12 pairs including lions, camels and elephants and statues of three civil or military officials in six pairs. At the north end of the Divine Boulevard there stands an archway called the "Gate of Divine Favor". Beyond the Gate of Divine Favor there are two marble bridges, and beyond the bridges we find a spoke of roads leading to the different Ming tombs. The Divine Boulevard, from the south end to the north, is more than 3,100 meters long.

Emperor Yong Le's tomb, or the Chang Mausoleum, features most prominently among the imperial tombs. Building of the tomb began in

Columns of nanmu in the Hall of Divine Favor.

The Hall of Divine Favor, the main structure of the Chang Mausoleum

1409, and took 11 long years to complete. In architectural style and ground plan, it is a reproduction of his father's tomb in Nanjing. The Chang Mausoleum consists of three courtyards. The courtyard in the front, which lies in between the gate of the mausoleum and the Gate of Divine Favor, has a few buildings that were used as warehouses of sacrificial objects. The main structure of the mausoleum, the Hall of Divine Favor, stands majestically in the courtyard in the middle. The hall, with a nine-bay front, features, among others, a roof as magnificent as the roof of the Hall of Supreme Harmony, the most important structure of the Forbidden City. What merits special mention is that the pillars are all of whole *nanmu*[6] tree trunks, and the thickest is 1.7 meters in diameter. Construction of the Hall of Divine Favor in the Chang Mausoleum was undertaken almost simultaneously with construction the Hall of Supreme Harmony, the former meant for use by the emperor after death and the latter, when he was alive. Both halls are on a three-layer marble platform and their roofs are of the highest status, thus providing a vivid example of how the principle "treating a dead person the same way as when the person is still alive" was followed. But life in the real world, after all, is more important than life in the nether world. That explains why the Hall of Divine Favor is smaller than the Hall of Supreme Harmony, and the platform on which it stands is not as high, and the courtyard in front of the platform is not as large as the courtyard in front of the Hall of Supreme Harmony. Behind the Hall of Divine Favor, in the third and the last courtyard, Emperor Yong Le's body lies in state, in a coffin buried beneath the so-called "Sacred City" with a pavilion-like watchtower in its front.

The Chang Mausoleum has never been opened, but the Ding Mausoleum shared by Emperor Shen Zong and his two queens has, allowing us to see what the underground part of an imperial tomb of the Ming Dynasty looks like. Emperor Shen Zong, who reigned supreme from 1573 to 1619, was the dynasty's 13th emperor, the second from the last. Construction of the Ding Mausoleum began in 1584 and, day after day, more than 30,000 soldiers and workmen toiled for six whole years to complete this underground palace. The construction cost came to a total of six million taels of silver, equivalent to two years' state revenue from the land tax.

The Ding Mausoleum is one of the largest of the 13 Ming Tombs. Unfortunately, most of its structures on the ground have perished, and the earthen mound or "Sacred City" and the watchtower in its front are the only structures that have survived the times. The underground part of the mausoleum lies 27 meters beneath the mound. It is, in fact, an underground palace complex consisting of three main halls and two side halls, which together occupy an area of 1,195 square meters. In between the halls there are passageways with stone doors. The walls are built with stone materials, and the floors, with quality bricks. The three main halls each have a double-leaf stone door. The doors are 3.3 meters high and 1.7 meters wide, each weighing about four tons. A door plate resembles something like a wedge, the part close to the heel post being 0.32 meters thick and the part at the other end, 0.17 meters, while both ends of the heel post are in the shape of bulbs for reduced friction. Archeologists were able to open the doors without much trouble thanks to their design that allows the gravity to shift onto the heal post. The hall in the rear, 36.1 meters long, 9.1 meters wide and 9.5 meters high, is the largest hall in the underground palace. Emperor Shen Zong's coffin is placed on a platform in the middle of the hall, and the queen's coffins are place at either side of it. Round the coffins there are large wooden trunks painted in bright red. Large quantities of burial objects - mostly things used by the tomb's occupiers in the real world - were found in the trunks - utensils of gold, silver and jade, porcelain articles, as well as garments of silk and brocade. Here is the dragon robe, the emperor's ceremonial dress, on which 12 twining dragons are embroidered. The queens' dresses feature embroidery of lively children, along with auspicious patterns of pine trees, bamboo plants and plum and peach flowers. The imperial crown is woven with fine, pure gold

Inside the Ding Mausoleum.

A member of the "imperial guard of honor" for the Ming Tombs.

threads, featuring a dragon with a pearl in its mouth and a phoenix decorated with flowers of precious stones. The two phoenix coronets belonging to the two queens are inlaid with 5,000 pearls and 100 precious stones each. Altogether, more than 3,000 burial objects were unearthed. Of these, the most valuable are the imperial crown and the phoenix coronets.

Imperial Tombs of the Qing Dynasty

The Qing Dynasty was the second — also the last — political regime set up by an ethnic minority group of China's to rule a unified China, following the Yuan Dynasty set up by the Mongols. The Manchurian rulers of the Qing Dyasty were keen to learn from the advanced culture of the Han majority ethnic group and the experiences of government from the Han rulers. To this end, they settled in the Forbidden City, the imperial complex of the Ming Dynasty, and inherited the Ming Dynasty's institutional rules and laws. Likewise, the imperial tombs of the Ming Dynasty were taken as models in construction of the Qing Dynasty's imperial tombs .

In 1644, Beijing became the capital of the Qing Dynasty. Not long after he was enthroned in the Forbidden City, Emperor Shun Zhi (1644-1661), the first Qing emperor to rule the entire China, followed the example of the Ming emperors and engaged himself in search of a site for his own tomb even though he was then a mere child. The site was finally decided, at the foot of the Yanshan Mountains in what is now Zunhua County, Hebei Province, to the northeast of Beijing. Emperor

The Yu Mausoleum, in the East Burial Ground of the Qing Dynasty in Zunhua County, Hebei Province.

Shun Zhi had his tomb built there, and so did his successor, Emperor Kang Xi. So the site became the "East Imperial Burial Ground of the Qing", relative to the "West Imperial Burial Ground of the Qing" in Yixian County, Hebei Province, to the west of Beijing. The East Imperial Burial Ground is home to tombs of five emperors, 15 crown empresses, and 130 imperial concubines, princes and princesses. Four emperors and 14 crown empresses, imperial concubines, princes and princesses were buried in the West Imperial Burial Ground.

In ground plan, the East Imperial Burial Ground is modeled after the 13 Ming Tombs, with the various tombs constructed under a unified plan while independent of one another. The largest tomb there belongs to Emperor Shun Zhi. A magnificent stone archway marks the entrance of the burial ground, and behind the archway there is the Divine Boulevard about 500 meters long, with stone statues standing at either side. Like the 13 Ming Tombs, the Divine Boulevard, along with the "imperial guard of honor" is meant for all the imperial tombs.

By tradition, children after death should be buried where their dead parents were buried. But Emperor Yong Zheng broke the convention and had his tomb built in the West Imperial Burial Ground, even though it is more than 100 kilometers away from the East Imperial Burial

The Zhao Mausoleum of the Qing Dynasty
in Shenyang, Liaoning Province

The West Burial Ground of the Qing Dynasty in Yixian County, Hebei Province.

Ground, where his grandfather and father were buried. He had personally chosen the site in Yixian, arguing that it was of an even higher geomantic quality. To justify his decision, the emperor quoted this and that classics to prove that it would be a blessing to the country if the imperial family had two burial grounds. As he had expected, nobody in the court dared to challenge his decision.

The next emperor, Emperor Qian Long, should have been buried at the side of his father's tomb in the West Imperial Burial Ground if the tradition was followed. In fact he had already chosen a site for his tomb there before he changed his mind, thinking that the East Imperial Burial Ground would eventually became a scene of destitution if his children and grandchildren, after their deaths, were buried in the West Imperial Burial Ground like him. So Emperor Qian Long had a tomb built in the East Imperial Burial Ground. Meanwhile, he issued an imperial decree to the effect that emperors that were to follow him should be built separately, alternately in the East Imperial Burial Ground and the West Imperial Burial Ground. In other words, if the father was buried in the East, the son should be buried in the West, and then the grandson, in the East. The rule of getting the father and son buried separately was followed for a period, but it was broken as two of the emperors in the late Qing period were buried with their fathers.

In ground plan, the two imperial burial grounds are identical. Emperor Qian Long died at 89, and occupied the throne for as long as 60 years. Under his reign, China enjoyed a long period of peace and prosperity, a period known to historians as the "flourishing age of Emperor Qian Long". Imposing and majestic as it is, his tomb, the Yu Mausoleum, is a vivid express expression of his complacence for his success. The underground part of the Yu Mausoleum consists of three halls with four doors, all built with stone. The door plates, altogether eight, are three meters high, 1.5 meters wide and 0.19 meters thick, weighing three tons each. A Buddhist Goddess of Mercy, standing barefooted on lotus flowers above clear ripples and wearing something that looks like a Western-style evening dress, is engraved on each plate. She has a crown of lotus flower petals on her head, and on her naked shoulders a shawl flutters in the gentle wind. The Goddess of Mercy is beautiful in shape, and her facial expressions are lively. The main hall in the underground palace complex features three sacred flowers on the ceiling, with Buddha engraved in the center of each flower which, along with inscriptions in Sanskrit, is surrounded by 24 petals. Texts of Buddhist sutras in Sanskrit are engraved on the walls, with Tibetan alphabets as phonetic symbols. The east and west walls, in particular, are engraved with images of Buddha and sacred objects of Buddhism. It is obvious that the underground palace complex enlivens what Emperor Qian Long, the self-styled "Old Man of Utter Perfection"[7], perceived of the Western Paradise, the "land of utter pleasure and happiness" where he hoped to stay after his death.

Emperors of the previous dynasties were invariably buried with their queens. In the Qing Dynasty, however, emperors and their queens were often buried in separate tombs. Under the court rules, the queen would share a tomb with her husband if she died earlier, and if she died after the emperor, a separate tomb would be built for her, at a site close to the emperor's tomb. Queens' tombs are, as a rule, smaller in size than emperors' tombs. The tomb of Empress Dowager Ci Xi (1835-1908) was the only exception. She was just one of the numerous concubines of Emperor Xian Feng (1831-1861). Because she mothered the emperor's only son, she was given the title "empress dowager" after her son assumed the throne. And as such, she was able to manipulate the child emperor and ran roughshod over the next emperor, also a child when ascending the dragon throne. She ordered rebuilding of her tomb so that it would be large and magnificent enough to suit her status as the country's *de facto* ruler. Now let's have a look at her mausoleum in the East Imperial Burial Ground. The Hall of Intense Benevolence, the main structure, and the two side halls are of precious hard timber. The beams bear patterns done with gold threads of the dragon, wind, clouds and the Chinese character 寿 (longevity). The walls are inlaid with auspicious patterns of the bat[8] – and the character 寿, which are produced by painstakingly putting bricks together.

What merits even greater attention, however, is the platform on which

Stone archways at the entrance of the West Burial Ground of the Qing Dynasty.

the Hall of Intense Benevolence stands. On those breast boards, a careful observer can count more than 100 engravings depicting the phoenix, the symbol of the queen, flying in the sky while the dragon, the symbol of the emperor, is trailing behind. Moreover, the tip of each rail post is carved into the shape of the phoenix, and beneath the legendary bird, on the rail post, a dragon is flying over the sea. Empress Dowager Ci Xi's mausoleum is the only place where the phoenix is pictured as assuming a higher status than the dragon.

Painted beams of the Hall of Intense Benevolence, the main structure for Empress Dowager Ci Xi's tomb in the East Burial Ground. Pay attention to the golden lines with which the decorative pattern and designs are done.

1. The Chinese Government has, since the 1950s, encouraged cremation of dead bodies to economize use of the country's land resources that are limited relative to the population. The traditional practice of burying dead bodies in the ground is virtually banned, but burial customs of ethnic minority groups are respected.

2. Visiting graves of elders and friends on the Qing Ming, the "festival" of the dead that falls on April 4, is still a folkway in modern China.

3. Wu Zetian (about 624-705) usurped the throne from her son in 690, but abducted in 705. She was the only female emperor throughout the Chinese history.

4. Zhu Yuanzhang or Emperor Taizu reigned supreme over China until he died in 1398.

5. In ancient times, celestial burials were popular among ethnic Mongolians as among ethnic Tibetans, both ethnic groups taking Lamaism as their religion.

6. Manmu is a precious hard timber that can be preserved almost indefinitely.

7. In late years, Emperor Qian Long, who took pride in his political and military achievements and his personal life characterized by luxury, peace, and many wives and consequently many children, called himself the "Old Man of Utter Perfection".

8. The bat is regarded as an auspicious animal, because in Chinese "bat" and "happiness" are homonyms.

Religious Buildings

Buddhism, Taoism and Islam were the main religions in ancient China,[1] each gathering a group of believers and performing a set of rituals at designated sites which, in this chapter, are referred to as "religious buildings".

Buddhist Buildings

Buddhism found its way from India into China in the first century AD by taking the Silk Road. At first, it was taken as a sort of witchcraft. Despite that, the religion was able to steadily build up its influence in the country with support of the Han Dynasty rulers. It boomed in a

A Buddhist temple in Zhoushan, Zhejiang Province.

historic period spanning from the fifth century to the sixth, a period when the country was torn apart by incessant wars and social upheavals. That period, known to historians as "period of the North and South Dynasties" (420-589), saw Buddhist temples spring up everywhere and Buddhist monks and nuns grow rapidly in numbers. According to historic records, the Liang, one of dynasties that ruled areas south of the Yangtze River, had 2,800 Buddhist temples and more than 50,000 monks and nuns. The Wei, one of the North Dynasties, had 30,000 temples and the number of monks and nuns exceeded two million. Buddhism enjoyed an even greater boom in the Tang Dynasty when full religious freedom was guaranteed. Under imperial decrees, translation of Buddhist texts became institutionalized, done at government-sponsored centers by Chinese and foreign monks who doubled as experts in Buddhism.

Buddhism was able to exert a profound influence on every aspect of social life in feudal China but never was it able to become the state religion. In fact none of the religions was. This is because Confucianism, as a complete system of philosophy and norms for social conduct, had already established itself as the dominating ideology. Meanwhile, ancient China was tolerant to all religious beliefs, irrespective of their origins, indigenous or alien, and people were quite indifferent toward the differences in doctrines of different religions. A person could be a believer of both Taoism and Buddhism while a faithful follower of Confucian teachings. In the course of its dissemination in China, Buddhism, constantly influenced by Confucianism, became a part of the Chinese culture, or Buddhism with Chinese characteristics. And so did Buddhist buildings, which came to assume the most striking characteristics of traditional Chinese architectural style.

Grottoes

Grottoes, as shrines for Buddha worshipping, were popular in the early period of Buddhism. These fall into two categories: those used by monks purely for self-cultivation, which feature altars for Buddha worshipping on the three walls, and those with a Buddhist tower inside

Buddhist statues in the Buddhist Fengxian Temple in Luoyang, Henan Province, which is actually one of the Longmen Grottoes.

for worshipping by the general public.

Ancient Chinese began building grottoes shortly after Buddhism found its way into China, and most grottoes that have been preserved to this day are found in Xinjiang, Gansu and Shaanxi of northwest China and Shanxi, Henan and Hebei in northern China. Like the religion itself, grottoes eventually became a part of the Chinese culture. In Dunhuang of Gansu and Datong of Shanxi, there are grottoes with carved pillars of stone in the center. These are invariably in the shape of Buddhist pagodas or Buddha images, with altars carved on them for worshipping. Grottoes built in later centuries feature carved Buddhist images on the wall facing the opening. But there are also grottoes that have Buddhist images on all the three walls, and round the images are colorful patterns of auspicious animals and plants, obviously to create the kind of environment which, Buddhist followers believed, was characteristic of the "Land of Buddha" or the "Land of Utter Happiness". Most grottoes found in China are of the second category.

Some grottoes are built on steep cliffs. Here is a quotation from an ancient Chinese author: "Half way from the blue sky, on those precipitous cliffs, one thousand caves are dug into rocks in which ten thousand altars of Buddha are worshipped. Though done with human labor, these arouse admiration for divine workmanship." Grottoes in such a natural environment seemed to be designed to hold Buddhist believers in awe of the mysterious "Land of Utter Happiness" and thus cement their devotion to Buddha. It won't be difficult to imagine that building of such grottoes was not an easy task in ancient times when everything had to be done by hand. One example is the Fengxian Temple, the largest Buddhist grotto in the area, which features a 17-meter tall Buddha statue carved on a hill. To facilitate the carving of the statue, workmen toiled for three whole years to cut open the hill and prepare the work site that was 41 meters deep into the hill and 36 meters wide. The first few grottoes on Mt. Maiji in Tianshui, Gansu Province, were built in the fourth century, and more were built in the following centuries. Altogether, some 200 grottoes are counted on the mountain, and most of the grottoes are on cliffs up to 100 meters high.

Grottoes on Mt. Maiji, Tianshui, Gansu Province.

A web of plank roads built on the surface of Mt. Maiji link the grottoes. The plank roads, somewhere between one and 1.5 meters wide and 800 meters in total length, are in 20 sections at different heights. In building a blank road, the first step was to hammer horizontal beams into the mountain, the distance in between the beams being half a meter to several meters, depending on the circumstances. When workmen were sure that the beams were fast enough, they would nail wooden planks to the "roadbed". The last step was to build the protective railings along the road. Building of the plank roads was already difficult enough, let alone the digging of the caves.

Grottoes are invaluable not only for their importance as Buddhist structures, but also as treasure houses of art. Inside grottoes we find large quantities of ancient Chinese carvings, clay sculptures and murals. Though on Buddhist themes, these artworks constitute a panorama of life in the real world. On murals found in the Dunhuang, Longmen and Yungang grottoes, for example, ancient buildings of all kinds are pictured - city walls, palaces, gardens, temples, marketplaces, streets, residential buildings, bridges, pavilions, towers, and so on, not only their physical outlooks but also their structures in minute details. These are of immense value to studies of ancient Chinese architecture. Moreover, grotto sculptures and murals feature prominently in the history of China's traditional fine art.

Buddhist Temples:

There were no temples in the country when Buddhism was first brought in. In most cases, Buddha worshipping was done in residences donated by ranking officials and other rich people who had converted to Buddhism. The principal hall, normally in the frontal courtyard, was used as the hall for Buddha worshipping, and buildings in the backyard, for preaching. A traditional residential or official complex always consists of buildings independent of one another, which are placed in a walled compound according to a certain order. And this kind of ground plan was to be followed in construction of Buddhist temples.

Subjects for worshipping became increasingly diverse as Buddhism

The Potala Palace in Lhasa.

spread, including not only Sakyamuni, founder of the religion, but also other Buddhas, as well as Bodhisattvas who are supposed to assist Buddha in enlightening the secular world, a whole army of guardian deities and numerous arhats or saints. So in addition to the Mahavira Hall where Sakyamuni is worshipped, Buddhist temples normally have the Hall of the Heavenly Kings[2], the Bodhisattvas Pavilion, the Hall of Arhats, as well as a number of auxiliary buildings. Like those in the Forbidden City, the main structures in a temple sit astride the axis of the compound. And these are arranged in order of the gate, the Hall of the Heavenly Kings, one or several halls dedicated to Buddha and his assistants, the Exoteric Hall, and the Tripitaka Pavilion (library of Buddhist texts). Flanking the main structures are less important buildings. Standing in order of bilateral symmetry at either side of the axis, these include the bell and drum towers at either side of the Hall of the Heavenly Kings, as well as dormitories, kitchens, etc., which are normally in the backyard. The main and auxiliary structures form several courtyards which, in some cases, are connected by galleries or verandas.

The Suspension Temple in Hunyuan County, Shanxi Province.

It is now clear that in ground plan, Buddhist temples in China are similar to traditional walled compounds. But there are exceptions. In the Jinghong Prefecture of southwest China's Yunnan Province, a Buddhist temple features the principal hall in the center, with a veranda leading to the gate, and round the principal hall there are pagodas, the Exoteric Hall, dormitories, etc. There is, however, no fixed order for the distribution of these structures, but the principal hall always faces east, because Sakyamuni is said to face east when, under the Pipal Tree of utter wisdom, attained Buddhahood through many years of fasting and meditation. In both architectural style and ground plan, the influence of Sthaviravada, a sect of Buddhism popular in the neighboring Myanmar and Thailand, is clearly visible in Buddhist temples in the Jinghong area.

Lamaseries in Tibet are often of an enormous size and irregular in ground plan. Almost the entire ethnic Tibetan people believe in Lamaism, and religious activities often draw thousands of participants.

In old Tibet, lamaseries performed some government functions and, in the course of religious activities, government decrees were often proclaimed in the name of Buddha. Because of the mass participation in religious activities, Buddhist halls have to be large. Tibet is situated on the Tibetan Plateau, the "roof of the world" that rises 4,500 meters above sea level, and most lamaseries are on mountain slopes or even sit atop mountains. Due to so rugged a terrain, it would have been impossible for Tibetans to build neat compounds like those walled temples or courtyards in other parts of China. The Potala Palace in Lhasa, capital of Tibet Autonomous Region, furnishes a most outstanding example of Buddhist shrines in Tibetan style.

Buddhism found its way into Tibet in the seventh century, and was eventually to develop into Lamaism - the Tibetan school of Buddhism - through centuries of struggle against the Ben, Tibet's primitive religion. Kublai (1215-1294), or Emperor Shi Zu of the Yuan Dynasty, conferred on Phatspa (1235-1280), a most revered Tibetan lama, the honorific title "National Teacher" and designated him to administer religious

The Mansuman Buddhist Temple at Jinghong prefecture, Yunnan Province.

and secular affairs in Tibet. This resulted in the establishment of a government combining political and religious powers that was to rule the region until the 1956 democratic reform after the founding of the People's Republic of China. Then came Tsong-Kha-Pa (1357-1419), founder of the Yellow Sect that was to develop into the mainstream of Tibetan Buddhism. Over the centuries, Lamaism has been the most important religion in areas inhabited by ethnic Tibetans including the entire Tibet Autonomous Region and parts of Sichuan and Qinghai provinces, as well as Inner Mongolia, home to ethnic Mongolians. While the most sacred shrine of Lamaism, the Potala Palace on Mt. M'buri in the center of Lhasa was the government palace of old Tibet.

The story goes back to the 7th century, when Tibet, or Tubo as it was referred to by ancient Chinese, witnessed its height of prosperity under the rule of King Songzan Gambo. For better political and economic relations, the Tang Dynasty and Tubo formed an alliance when Li Shimin, the second emperor of the Tang Dynasty, married Princess Wen Cheng to King Songzan Gambo. Then the king ordered construction of a palace on Mt. M'buri for the princess.[3] Construction on Mt. M'buri continued after the royal coupled died, as lamas in increasing numbers came to dwell and practice their religion on Mt. M'buri. Then in the mid-17th century, massive reconstruction was done after the fifth Dalai Lama received official recognition from the imperial court of the Qing Dynasty. Most of the buildings in the present-day Potala Palace were build under the fifth Dalai Lama. The 13-story main structure of the Potala Palace is 117 meters high and 400 meters wide from east to west. Inside the palace complex there is a complete array of structures built at different heights of the slope — palace halls, halls for Buddha worshipping, the hall where the Dalai Lamas studied Buddhist texts, the hall where pagodas dedicated to the Dalai Lamas are kept for worshiping, as well as courtyards. These are divided into the Red Palace, *alias* the hall of the Dalai Lamas' pagodas in the center of the complex, and the White Palace — bedchambers, halls for Buddha worshipping, the hall where the Dalai Lamas studied Buddhist texts, etc. The roof ridges are all plated in gold which, dazzling under the sun, add glory, magnificence and mystery to the palace complex.

Complete freedom from all worldly disasters, worries and misgivings in the "Land of Utter Happiness" is the ultimate pursuit of Buddhist devotees. And to be immortal in the "Land of Utter Happiness", one should, through self-cultivation, free oneself from all worldly desires by practicing austerity in places far away from the mortal world. For this reason, most Buddhist temples are found deep in mountains and other secluded places. As time goes by, many mountains with temples have become scenic sites known in China and abroad, including Mt. Wutai in Shanxi, Mt. E'mei in Sichuan, Mt. Jiuhua in Anhui, and Mt. Putuo in Zhejiang.[4]

Buddha Halls:

Buddhist halls vary in size, some with a three- or five-bay front while the most imposing halls may have a nine-bay front, almost as large as a palace hall. A hall can be home to just one sculpture — in

The giant Buddha in Leshan, Sichuan Province.

most cases the sculpture of Sakyamuni. But there are also halls in which Sakyamuni is worshipped along with a range of other Buddhist deities, and the sculptures can be placed either in the center or at the side of the wall facing the gate. Built in 857, the principal hall in the Temple of Buddhist Glory on Mt. Wutai is the oldest of its kind preserved to this day. The hall, with a seven-bay front, is 34 meters wide and 17.6 meters long. And inside the hall there is a raised platform on which more than 30 sculptures — of Sakyamuni and his assistants — are placed.

Thanks to development of clay sculpturing, metallurgical and paint production techniques, taller and larger Buddhist sculptures became increasingly preferred, hence construction of halls large and high. A typical example is the Goddess of Mercy Pavilion in the Temple of Solitary Delight in Jixian County of Tianjin Municipality, which was built in 984. The pavilion, in fact a magnificent hall with a three-part exterior that resembles a three-story building, is 22.5 meters high. In the center of the hall there stands a sculpture of the Goddess of Mercy measured at 16 meters from head to foot, and to see her face, one has to look up, bending one's neck backward as far as possible. The hall would be pitched dark but for the windows on the upper part of the wall through which light is allowed in to illuminate the head of the sculpture, thus making the environment even more mysterious. Even larger and taller is the Hall of Supreme Wisdom in the Temple of Universal Peace in Chengde, Hebei Province. Inside the hall there stands a 24.12 meter-tall sculpture of the Bodhisattva with One Thousand Hands and One Thousand Eyes. Round the sculpture there is a cone-shaped platform of three layers, which allows people to view the statue at different heights and from different angles.

The largest Buddha statue in China — nay, throughout the world — is cut from a whole cliff that overlooks the Dadu River flowing past its foot, at the Temple of Rising Clouds in Leshan, Sichuan Province. The Leshan Giant Buddha is 71 meters high. Its shoulders are measured at

A Buddhist temple at Chengde, the imperial
summer resort of the Qing Dynasty.

24 meters each, and its nose a long as five meters. It took 90 years, from 713 to 803, for workmen and artists to complete the terrific job of carving the cliff into the giant Buddha, along with construction of a seven-story pavilion in the front to facilitate viewing of the giant Buddha. The pavilion was destroyed in fire in the Ming Dynasty. A full view of the world wonder is possible from a boat sailing midstream of the Dadu River.

Buddhist towers:

As religious shrines, pagodas and towers, which originate from India, are unique to Buddhism. Sakyamuni is said to have his body cremated after he died, and his disciples found in his ashes numerous holy relics — hard, bright pearl-like things that were material testimony to his attainment of utter wisdom and enlightenment.[5] The holy relics were then divided, sent to different places and, for worshipping, buried in stupas — earthen mounds in the shape of a semi-circle with an umbrella-

Temple of Solitary Delight in Jixian County of Tianjin Municipality.

The famous wooden tower at the Buddha Palace
Temple in Yingxian County, Shaxi Province.

like object on the top, which constituted the earliest form of Buddhist towers.

Like Buddhism itself, stupas in China eventually became incorporated with the Chinese culture, culminating in pagodas and towers with distinct Chinese characteristics. Towers in their earliest form have all perished, but stone engravings excavated from Han Dynasty tombs provide us with full pictures of such structures. These are, in fact, multi-story buildings open on all sides for a full view of what is below and all around in the distance, with inter-connected verandas round each floor for ascending and descending. As Buddhism was gaining influence, stupas became high towers, as people believed that holy relics found in ashes of Buddhist saints should be placed high. As time went by, "stupa towers", so to speak, underwent constant changes in structure and style and came to be established as an important

The Double Towers in the Temple of Arhats, Suzhou, Jiangsu Province.

part of China's traditional architectural art.

Most Buddhist towers in China resemble a multistory building in traditional style. The earliest of such towers are wooden structures modeled after secular structures. The oldest Buddhist tower of timber is in the Buddha Palace Temple in Yingxian County, Shaxi Province.

The Sakyamuni Pagoda, an octagonal structure 67.3 meters high, was built in 1056. One may take it as a five-story structure before getting into it. But once inside, one will find that it actually has nine floors with winding terraces and Buddhist sculptures placed on every floor for worshipping. The wooden tower is still in good shape even though in the past 900 years, several major tremors have struck the area.

Wooden structures are liable to catch fire, and high-rise wooden structures, in particular, face the danger of being struck by lightning. In view of this problem, ancient Chinese engineers and workmen developed a kind of Buddhist towers built with both timber and bricks — brick towers with a wooden "coat" that makes the structures look traditional in style. In case of a fire, the wooden "coat" may be destroyed but the tower itself will remain intact. Brick-timber towers are found mostly in south China. One example is the Pagoda of Dragon Glory in Shanghai, a seven-story octagonal structure built in 977. The Cloud Rock Temple in Suzhou, Jiangsu Province, also a seven-story octagonal structure, was built in 961 and its wooden "coat" was destroyed in fire a long time ago. The brick tower, however, is known as the "Chinese leaning tower" though it may not be as famous as the Leaning Tower of Pisa. Fortunately, the tower has stopped declining thanks to measures

The Fengshui Tower in Xinye Village, Jiande County, Zhejiang Province.

taken by Chinese engineers to strengthen its foundation with concrete.

Buddhist towers built entirely of bricks or stone can also be found in China. Among these fireproof structures, the best known is the Pagoda of Perfect Purity in Tiantai, Zhejiang Province, which was built in 598. Some Buddhist towers are coated with glazed tiles all over, such as the Pavilion of Buddha Fragrance on the Longevity Hill in the Summer Palace, Beijing.

In China, there are towers that architects choose to call "close-eave structures". The ground floor of such a tower is always the highest, while the upper floors are low, in fact as low as possible, so the eaves of the different stories are close to one another. "Close-eave" towers are mostly brick structures, in the shape of a square, hexagon or octagon. The earliest "close-eave" towers were built in the Tang Dynasty, which were to become popular in north China in the Song Dynasty. There are differences between those of the Tang Dynasty and those of the succeeding dynasties. "Close-eave" towers built in the Tang Dynasty are in the shape of a square, with staircases inside for ascending and descending. In comparison, those built after the Tang Dynasty are mostly octagonal in shape and are solid, thus denying ascending and descending from inside. Moreover, the ground floor is on a raised platform, the walls and the platform both beautiful with Buddha images and floral and animal designs. Even though nobody can enter a "close-eave" tower, artificial doors and windows are carved on the wall of each floor, which are also exquisitely decorated. Moreover, the eaves are constructed in such a way as to resemble those of traditional structures of timber. The Pagoda in the Temple of Celestial Tranquility in Beijing is a best representative of the "close-eave" towers.

Pagodas found in areas inhabited by ethnic Tibetans are markedly different from those found elsewhere in the country. Ethnic Tibetans believe in Lamaism, and pagodas in ethnic style of theirs are often referred to as "lama pagodas". These are white structures, resembling an alms bowl placed upside down, and on it top there is a large, round structure containing the ashes of a revered lama. During the Yuan Dynasty, large numbers of "Lama pagodas" were built in China's heartland, as the dynasty's Mongol rulers were Lamaism devotees. One of the best known "lama pagodas" is found in the Temple of Divine

The Pagoda in the Temple of Celestial Tranquility in Beijing is a best representative of the "close-eave" towers. It was built in the 12th century.

The "white pagoda" in the Temple of Celestial Tranquility, Beijing. It is one of the best known "lama pagodas".

Response, Beijing. The pagoda, designed by a Nepalese architect, was built in 1221.

Buddhism found its way into different parts of China at different historic periods. Besides, ethnicity, cultural background and natural conditions vary from region to region in so vast a country. As time went by, three schools of the religion came into being: the Han ethnic school of Buddhism, the Tibetan school of Buddhism and the Sthaviravada school of Buddhism. People of the Dai ethnic group living in south Yunnan province believe in the Sthaviravada school of Buddhism that originates from the neighboring Thailand and Myanmar, and Buddhist towers there are generalized as "Myanmar pagodas" for an architectural style popular in parts of southeast Asia, Myanmar in particular. The Manlong Flying Pagodas, which were built in 1204 in what is now Damenglong of Jinghong in Yunnan Province, is a typical example of such structures. These nine pagodas form a neat group. The principal pagoda, 16.29 meters high, stands in the middle, round which eight smaller pagodas, all 9.1 meters high, form a circle. The nine pagodas, like a grove of bamboo shoots, roughly are of the same shape and architectural style as "lama pagodas" — the main part standing on a raised platform with an alms bowl-like structure placed upside down on its top.

When Buddhism was first introduced to China, pagodas were always

The Manlong Flying Pagodas, which were built in 1204 in what is now Damenglong of Jinghong in Yunnan Province.

built in the center of a temple. As time went by, Buddhist sculptures replaced pagodas as the sacred subjects for worshipping and, in temples, pagodas were often built in front of the principal hall or behind it, forming the so-called "pagoda courtyards". While becoming increasingly diverse in architectural style, Buddhist towers, including pagodas, were no longer purely religious structures. The Wild Goose Pagoda in Chang'an, capital of the Tang Dynasty, became famous not only as a religious shrine but also as the venue for gatherings of successful candidates in imperial examinations for officialdom. After the results of an imperial examination were announced, those candidates who had emerged victors would, individually or in groups, ascend the pagoda and write poems on the walls along with their autographs — obvious to make themselves remembered eternally. The Six-Harmony Pagoda stands majestically on a hill overlooking the Qiantang River in Zhejiang Province. In ancient times, lanterns hung from its flying eaves

The Ahat Pagodas in the Temple of Great Awakening, Beijing.

would be lit at night to direct boats sailing in the river.

Buddhist towers and pagodas add glory to Buddhist shrines which, as we have said, are mostly in places of seclusion noted for scenic beauty. This has inspired the Chinese to build towers that blend in natural beauty of scenic spots, towers that have nothing to do with religion.

Taoist Structures

Taoism began rising in about the second century. It practices an elaborate array of religious rituals, including the daily chanting of Taoist sutras, sacrificial ceremonies dedicated to various gods, goddess and immortals, and rites performed to save the souls of the dead or beg Heaven for blessing to believers. Taoism is an indigenous religion, and Taoist structures are, in the main, traditional in architectural style and ground plan. Despite that, Taoist structures are unique in many ways, relative to palace structures and Buddhist shrines.

Taoists believe that a person could become immortal through practice of austerities and that immortal dwell in places of seclusion with surpassing natural beauty, deep in mountains or on islands on high seas. For this reason, Taoist temples are found mostly in mountains noted for scenic beauty, in order that followers can put their trust in nature and thus transcend the worldly. As a matter of fact, some of the most beautiful mountains, such as Mt. Qingcheng in Sichuan and Mt. Wudang in Hubei, are at the same time the best-known Taoist shrines. Taoists also believe that immortals like to live in high-rise buildings in order to be close to the Heavenly Palace. That may explain why Taoist structures are mostly multistory structures. The Chinese for a Taoist temple of the normal size is " 观 " (pronounced as "guan"), meaning "pavilion" or "multistory building" when used as a noun and "look upward" when used as a verb. Larger Taoist temples are called " 宫 " (pronounced as "gong"), meaning "palace", and smaller Taoist temples, " 道院 " (pronounced as "dao yuan"), meaning "Taoist courtyard". Whether a "palace" or a simple courtyard, a Taoist shrine invariably features buildings dedicated to immortals. Here are some of the most

The Azure Cloud Temple on Mt. Taishan, a most important Taoist shrine.

common names for such buildings — Pavilion for Welcoming Immortals, Pavilion for Gathering Immortals, and Pavilion of Ten Thousand Immortals.

Taoists attribute the founding of their religion to Lao Zi, a philosopher who was active about 2,500 years ago, and take his *Scripture of Ethics* (*Dao De Jing*), as the central text of the Taoist doctrines. Meanwhile, Taoism is a polytheist religion, and it worships countless gods, goddesses and deities, each supposedly performing a specific function or duty to the benefit of the mortal world. The Dragon King, for example, can be counted on for rain while punishing people with flooding when he is angry. One may go to Lord Guan for protection from disasters and misfortunes. The God of Medicine is supposedly to have the magic power to make patients recover. If you want to get rich, well, beg the God of Wealth for blessing. The Ma Zu Goddess, the protector of sailors and travelers sailing the turbulent seas, has been worshipped not only by people in China's coastal regions but also by overseas Chinese in practically all parts of the world. In a Taoist temple we may find numerous gods, goddess and deities being worshipped. In most case, Taoist temples follow the same ground plan as traditional compounds, the principal hall sitting astride the axis of the compound while less important structures are placed at either side, in symmetrical order.

Islamic Structures

Islam was brought into China in the mid-7th century. Islamic rituals are performed in mosques, which are different from structures of all the other religions in architectural style and decoration.

Moslems revere Allah as the only God. Allah is invisible but makes His presence anywhere and any time, and Moslems are, therefore, opposed to idolatry. Unlike shrines of other religions where idols are invariably worshipped, no idols or sacrifices are allowed in mosques. Moslems just perform religious services in the direction of Mecca, the holiest shrine of Islam. Mecca lies to the west of China, and that's why Chinese Moslems always face west when performing religious services. No matter where a mosque is, its gate always faces east. On the west wall facing the gate, there is a passage in Arabic from the Holy Koran, and round the quotation there are exquisitely decorated borders. Once in, a Moslem will instantly know the right direction for prayers.

Mosque of Tongxin County, Ningxia Hui Autonomous Region.

In China, mosques fall into two major types — those resembling traditional halls and those in Arab style. The minaret is the landmark structure for any mosque, from the top of which Azans call Moslems to gather for collective prayers. Some mosques are fitted with a library of the Holy Koran and Islamic classics, as well as the Imam's office rooms, bedrooms, etc. The interior and exterior of mosques are invariably decorated with patterns formed by texts in Arabic in praise of Allah and Mohammed the Prophet, as well as decorative designs formed with geometric or plant figures.

Arab and Persian merchants who came to China for business played a big role in promoting the spreading of the religion in the country. This was true especially in the period spanning from the seventh century to the 12th, when trade between China and Arab countries flourished. Of the Mosques built during that period, some are still in good shape, and these are clearly the same kind of Islamic structures popular in the Arab world today. Mosques built in the following centuries, however, are predominantly Chinese in architectural style and ground plan and turn out to be walled compounds consisting of several courtyards with the prayer hall and other main structures sitting on the axis. The gate of such a mosque is usually a large, pavilion-like structure of timber, often with an archway in its front. Minarets are also structures of timber. Minarets in the earliest Chinese mosques are stone or brick structures, like those in the Arab world. As time went by, minarets became pavilion-like structures of timber. Halls of conventional size are often too small for collective prayers on Friday, the Djumah, which Moslems attend as a religious duty. In some mosques, parallel halls are therefore connected for religious services.

The Uygurs, who live in compact communities in Xinjiang of China's far northwest, are the country's second largest ethnic Moslem group, following the Huis. While largely Arabic in architectural style, their mosques bear characteristics that stem from natural conditions of the

The prayer hall of Atkar Mosque. Pay attention to
the elaborate patterns on the wall and ceiling.

Atkar Mosque in Keshi, Xinjiang.

area and are conditioned by locally available construction materials. Minarets that stand majestically at the side of mosques are often landmark structures. The arched roofs of the prayer halls are as eye-catching, and so are the arched gates and verandas with pinnacles. The structures, taken as a whole, are simple and sprightly in style, but a careful observer won't miss those bright, elaborate decorations on different parts of a structure. Gates of mosques and altars in prayer halls are exquisite artworks with floral decorations of gypsum to which paints are applied. Even walls surrounding mosques are carved with decorative designs and patterns with passages in praise of Allah and the Prophet.

1. Nestorianism, a Christian sect, was introduced to China in the seventh century, but before long it came to extinct. It was until the early 1800s did the various sects of Christianity become able to spread in China.

2. Heavenly Kings are the greatest Buddha guardians.

3. The king and princess have always been remembered for their pioneering role in promoting the relations between Tibet and the rest of China. Their statues are still worshipped in the centuries-old Cave of King of Dharma on Mt. M'buri.

4. These are collectively referred to as the "four most sacred mountains of China's", which are reputed not only as Buddhist shrines but also for their natural beauty.

5. It is said that the ashes of Buddhist saints — monks who have attained utter wisdom — also contain such holy relics. As a rule, these, too, are buried in stupas for worshipping.

Traditional Chinese Gardens

Ancient gardens constitute an independent branch of China's traditional architectural art. They are, in fact, artworks created through renovation or imitation of natural scenery. As places of rest and recreation, a typical Chinese garden comprises "four basic elements" - mountains and rivers whether real or man-made, buildings such as pavilions and corridors, and plants. These are artistically arranged along with roads and trails for a unique visual beauty and an atmosphere of tranquility and peace. Art objects, furniture and decorative objects are an indispensable part of a garden, as these demonstrate not only the purpose of the garden but also the personal taste, literary attainment and social status of its owner.

Ancient Chinese gardens fall into numerous types, varying from one another in size and style. Imperial gardens are large in size while limited in numbers, including, for example, the Summer Palace in Beijing and the Mountainous Summer Resort in Chengde, Hebei Province. Large-sized scenic spots are often regarded as gardens as well — to be more precise, as " 园林 " (pronounced as "yuan lin"), or "gardens in forests". These include Mt. Taishan and Mt. Huangshan on the UNESCO List of World Heritage, which are reputed for a perfect combination of invaluable natural landscapes and landscapes of humanity. Mt. Putuo in Zhejiang, Mt. E'mei in Sichuan, Mt.Wutai in Shanxi and Mt. Jiuhua in Anhui are the four sacred mountains of Chinese Buddhism, featuring centuries-old temples, lush-green forests and exotic rocks in an environment so peaceful and senile as to hold people in awe of Buddha. Private gardens found in areas south of the Yangtze River were, in fact, indispensable parts of high-class mansions. These gardens vary in area, from several hectares to less than one third of a hectare. Whether large or small, a private garden invariably has a pond and an artificial hill built with earth from digging of the pond as well as pavilions and bridges — an expression of the owner's pursuit of harmony between what is natural and what is man-made. Growing pot flowers and planting trees in courtyards are the hobby of hundreds of millions. People like to make their homes garden-like, so long as there is space to spare for decoration with exotic rocks, trees, flowers or, most preferably, a small pond.

Ancient Chinese Gardens

The earliest " 园林 " or "gardens in forests" came into being in the Shang period (21st century BC-16th century BC) as pleasure grounds for aristocrats. These were, in fact, natural sites enclosed for hunting. There were no structures built with human labor at such sites, except a few raised platforms on which people stood for a better view of the

A typical garden of traditional style, which comprises a pool, rocks in exotic shapes, plants and buildings such as pavilions and halls.

scenery. As time went by, palace structures were built and ponds dug for angling in "gardens in forests" to better satisfy the needs of aristocrats for hunting, recreation and banqueting. In both the Qin and Han dynasties, even larger "gardens in forests" were developed along with construction of palace complexes. The Weilin Garden, the imperial garden of the Han Dynasty, was a vast expanse of rolling mountains, deep forests and winding rivers, stretching for well over 150 kilometers outside the capital city, Chang'an. In addition to animals and plants, the garden had clusters of palace buildings.

From the third to the sixth century, China experienced a period of incessant internal wars and conflicts. The country split into three independent kingdoms — the Wei, Shu and Wu — after the Han Dynasty collapsed in 220. Through nearly half a century's war, rulers of the Wei unified China in 265 under what is known to historians as the West Jin Dynasty. Then, in 317, a new dynasty, the East Jin, replaced the West Jin. Right after the East Jin collapsed in 420, China split again. In areas south of the Yangtze River, four dynasties overturned one another in succession through bloody wars and, in the north, five dynasties ruled in succession, before China was unified again in 581, under the Sui Dynasty. Bitterly disappointed and disillusioned, members of the intelligentsia tried to evade the reality by finding a spiritual sustenance in the natural world, hence the popularity of landscape paintings and poetry depicting natural scenery in what is known as the period of "Wei- Jin and South-North Dynasties". Many of them also tried to make where they lived "natural" by planting trees and flowers, building artificial hills and digging streams, and this marked the beginning for construction of gardens in their true sense. Meanwhile, changes began taking place in imperial "gardens in forests", where man-made landscapes were added with construction of pavilions and building of artificial hills.

Under the Tang Dynasty, China experienced an unprecedented economic and cultural boom. Consequently, gardening thrived along

Deep in the Mt. Emei, a leading scenic spot in China.

with construction of imperial palace structures. As a matter of fact, gardens were an indispensable part of the palace complexes in Chang'an, the national capital. Behind the Daming Palace, the largest palace complex, there was the Celestial Lake with a man-made isle modeled after what Taoists described as Penglai, a dwelling place of immortals on the high seas. On festival occasions, people would gather at a public pleasure ground set up by the government along the Qujiang River that snaked through the northern suburbs of the city. Public pleasure grounds were also found in other major cities, including Hangzhou in east China and the southwest city of Guilin. As regional inspector of Hangzhou, Bai Juyi (772-846), better known as a most important poet of the Tang Dynasty, did a lot to develop the West Lake scenic area in the city.[1] In his late years, the poet, now stripped of all official posts, settled in Luoyang, central China, where he had a residence built for himself. The residence occupied an area of 17 mu (about 667 square meters in one mu). Housing and other buildings accounted for one third of the area, bamboo groves, for one ninth, and a pond, for one fifth. Though not large, the pond had three islets and, on each of the islets, there was a pavilion. Meanwhile, trails were built round the pond and through the bamboo groves, and lotus and water chestnut were grown in the pond. Here and there in the courtyard there were pavilions and corridors, where the poet did reading in solicitude or met friends for poetry recitation, dining and wining. Artificial hills added beauty and taste to the garden-like residence, and so did rocks from places far away, such as Lake Taihu about 1,000 kilometers to the southeast of Luoyang. The courtyard-garden took ten long years to build, where everything was painstaking planned.

Gardening became even more popular in the Song Dynasty. Just in Bianliang (the present-day Kaifeng, Henan Province), the national capital, there were nine imperial gardens. Of these, the largest and most magnificent was built during the reign of Emperor Hui Zong (1082-1135). The emperor, who couldn't be worse in managing state affairs but excelled in painting and calligraphy, ordered building, in the Yinyue Garden, of true-to-life imitations of all the major mountains, lakes and

Picture shows the White Pagoda on the Jade Islet in the Beihai Lake, which stands on the commanding height of the former imperial winter palace.

rivers across China. Attention was paid to every minute detail, including even those terraced trails cut on mountains and plank roads winding round cliffs on riverbanks. A government office was specially set up in Suzhou to collect exotic plants and rocks for use in the imperial garden. More often than not, these were forcibly taken away without payment. No wonder public anger kept mounting when construction of the garden was in progress.

Court ministers and other aristocrats, on their part, were no less crazy. More than 100 upper class gardens were eventually counted in and round Bianliang as the craze went from bad to worse. Meanwhile, garden-like restaurants and pleasure boats were becoming increasingly common. Horticulture thrived as a side-product of the construction boom, and large numbers of gardeners and garden designers came forth. Luoyang, a major city to the west of Bianliang, was the national center of horticulture, where gardeners and horticulturists developed nearly 1,000 varieties of plants by using hybridization, domestication and other techniques. These included, in particular, peony of more than 100 varieties, for which the city has been famed until today as the "kingdom of peonies".

Gardening continued to boom in the Ming and Qing dynasties spanning from the late 14th century to the early 20th. Ancient gardens that we can still enjoy were mostly built during that period.

Imperial Gardens of the Qing Dynasty

Feudal China once again enjoyed a period of peace and economic prosperity under emperors Kang Xi, Yongzheng and Qianlong of the Qing Dynasty, who reigned supreme in succession from the late-17th century to the late 18th. Emperors Kang Xi and Qian Long, in particular, were no longer content with the imperial garden enclosed in the Forbidden City, and ordered construction of imperial gardens outside the capital city. The northwest suburbs of Beijing with rolling hills and winding rivers came to be chosen, where some palaces had already been built in the Yuan and Ming dynasties as temporary imperial abodes. On that basis, construction began on order of Emperors Kang Xi on what was to eventually become known as "five gardens on three hills".[2] Besides, a string of smaller gardens were built for imperial princes on Beijing's northwest suburbs.[3] Construction continued under Emperor Qian Long and, by the mid-19th century, the area, about 20 kilometers

The Mountainous Summer Resort in Chengde, Hebei Province.

Picture shows a part of the Garden of Perfect Splendor, which was reduced to ruins by British and French troops in the mid-1800s.

in circumference, had come to boast a concentration of imperial gardens unprecedented in scale and splendor.

In 1703, under Emperor Qian Long, construction began on the Mountainous Summer Resort in Chengde a few hundred kilometers to the north of Beijing, which was to proceed almost simultaneously with construction and expansion projects on Beijing's northwest suburbs. Chengde, which lies to the north of the Great Wall where it is much cooler in Summer than in Beijing, used to be an imperial hunting ground. The Mountainous Summer Resort, with an area of 500 square kilometers, is the largest imperial garden of the Qing Dynasty. It has a complete range of palace buildings that provided the same ease and comfort to emperors as when they were in Beijing, including some where emperors would continue working on state affairs. There are altogether 72 scenic spots in the walled resort. The scenic spots fall into two types — lakeside spots and spots in forests and mountains. Round the resort eight Buddhist temples were built on imperial orders, including some lamaseries in Tibetan style. The resort and the temples are now on the UNESCO List of World Heritage.

The Garden of Perfect Splendor and the Garden of Clear Ripples (or the Summer Palace known to Westerners), however, are seen as most important for their artistic and historic value. Here is a brief account of the two imperial gardens:

The Garden of Perfect Splendor:

At its full grandeur, the Garden of Perfect Splendor was known in the West as the "garden of all gardens" before it was set ablaze by an allied force of British and French troops in the mid-1900s.

The Garden of Pleasant Spring was the first imperial garden built under Emperor Kang Xi in Beijing's northwest suburbs. To be more precise, it was the first imperial abode built there. As such, it is divided into two parts. The frontal part consisted of palace buildings for work and dwelling of his majesty, and the part in the rear is a lakeside garden.

The Garden of Perfect Splendor was built in 1708, also on order of Emperor Kang Xi, which he gave to Prince Yong, his fourth son, whom he had discreetly designated as his successor. Prince Yong was

The Garden of Tranquility and Appropriateness on the Fragrance Hill, Beijing.

The Palace of Nationwide Peace and Order, a scenic spot in the Garden of Perfect Splendor, as pictured by an imperial artist. The palace no longer exists.

enthroned as the new emperor, Emperor Yong Zheng, after his father's death. During his reign, he ordered construction of more palaces in the garden to expand it into one more imperial abode on the northwest suburb of the capital. Expansion of the Garden of Perfect Splendor continued under the next emperor, Emperor Qian Long, under whose rule China underwent one more period of peace and prosperity. The emperor, who took pride in what historians refer to as the "Qian Long's era of national boom", was a man of literary attainment and he was, in particular, fond of gardening. In his lifetime, he went on six inspection tours of China's richest areas in the south, in the course of which he was able to visit numerous scenic spots and private gardens. The visits inspired him to order expansion of the Garden of Perfect Splendor by having the Garden of Pleasant Spring and the Garden of Eternal Spring incorporated into it.

The project took 30 long years to complete. Lakes and ponds dotted an area of 350 hectares occupied by the expanded Garden of Perfect Splendor, which is also known as the "Three Gardens of Perfect Splendor". The largest is the Sea of Happiness, which is 600 meters wide. The lake, also the largest scenic spot in the garden, featured an islet that symbolizes the Immortals' Island on the high seas. There were also lakes or ponds two or three hundred meters wide. Most of the water bodies, however, were even smaller, forming scenic spots together with palace courtyards or man-made hills in their front or behind. A web of streams linked the lakes and ponds, making the various scenic spots parts of an integral whole while independent of one another. Lakes, ponds and streams accounted for half of the area, and hills, for about one fifth. Built with earth from digging of lakes and ponds, none of the hills were high enough to spoil the scenery characterized by ripples dancing in lakes on a vast expanse of flatland. Instead, they were indispensable parts of each and every scenic spot by adding beauty to the Garden of Perfect Splendor as a whole.

The Garden of Perfect Splendor comprises numerous smaller gardens scattering all over the place, in lakes and ponds or right at their side. It is smaller in area than the Garden of Clear Ripples on Beijing's northwest suburb and the Beihai Lake in the city center. Moreover, it does not have a landmark building or commanding scenic spot like the Buddha Fragrance Pavilion atop the Hill of Longevity in the Garden of Clear Ripples and the White Pagoda on the Jade Islet in the Beihai Lake. The scenic beauty, however, is unique in that even though scattering, the different scenic spots form a united whole. On order of Emperor Qian Long, imitations of famous scenic spots in south China were built in the garden — for example, the "Three Moons Reflected in Water" and the "Autumn Moon in the Lake" in the West Lake scenic area of Hangzhou. Believe it or not, there was even a "shopping street" named after the scenic city Suzhou to which the emperor took a special liking. On festival occasions, Emperor Qian Long and the emperors after him would, accompanied by court ministers and taking with them their wives and concubines, visit the Suzhou Street and "buy" from eunuchs and court ladies who disguised themselves as traders.

Altogether, buildings in 120 clusters were counted in the garden before it was destroyed in the Second Opium War. With a combined construction space of 160,000 square meters, these were all scenic spots of surpassing beauty. Included were the Hall of Honesty and Brightness where the emperor granted audiences to court ministers, the Jade Pavilion built as a symbol of the immortals' dwelling place, and Palace of Blessings where imperial ancestral tablets were worshipped. Unlike the Forbidden City where the structures are stereotyped in architectural style and always placed in rigidly symmetrical order, buildings in the Garden of Perfect Splendor were much livelier, with diverse architectural planes in the shape of H or of Chinese characters 工 and

Ruins of a European-style structure in the Garden of Perfect Splendor.

田 , or the carpenter's square, or fan-shaped, in addition to neat squares and rectangles. Pavilions were also diverse in shape - square, hexagonal, octagonal, cross-shaped or circular. There were corridors winding round lakes, snaking up and down the artificial hills, or running straight to connect courtyards or halls. On order of Emperor Qian Long, a group of stone structures in Western style were built in the Garden of Perfect Splendor, featuring fountains, sculptures and neatly pruned plants like those in European gardens. Designed by Guiseppe Castiglione, an Italian missionary and architect, these were the first Western-style buildings ever constructed in China.

Allied forces of British and French troops set the Garden of Perfect Splendor afire and looted its treasures after they captured Beijing in 1860, during the Second Opium War. The "garden of all gardens" was reduced to a vast expanse of rubble, leaving just a few broken columns and archways of stone to serve as material testimony to the humiliation

A bird's-eye-view of the Summer Palace.

The Hill of Longevity seen from the opposite bank of the Kunming Lake, Summer Palace.

inflicted by the imperialist powers on China and her people. For an idea of how the garden looked like at the time of its full grandeur, we now have to count on historic records and paintings left over from the imperial archives.

The Garden of Clear Ripples:

Construction of the garden was completed in 1764, and had its name changed into the Garden of Peace and Harmony in 1888 which, in the West, is better known as the Summer Palace.

After completion of the Garden of Perfect Splendor in 1744, Emperor Qian Long wrote an article which, while giving a description of the garden's beauty and magnificence, demanded that his descendents stop wasting the country's human and financial resources on gardens. But just a few years afterwards he forgot what he had said and ordered construction of the Garden of Clear Ripples not far to the west of the Garden of Perfect Splendor. The emperor was fond of those private gardens he had visited during his inspection tours of southern China. These gardens, he had found, featured natural scenery of rolling hills and winding rivers and streams. In comparison, the Garden of Tranquility and Appropriateness on the Fragrance Hill and the Garden of Light and Tranquility on the Jade Spring Hill did not have a lake or a river. The Garden of Perfect Splendor, as the emperor saw it, was not really perfect in that it does not have hills even though it is beautiful

The Gate of Benevolence and Longevity, the main gate of the imperial abode in the Summer Palace.

The south slope of the Longevity Hill.

with lakes and ponds. It so happened that in between the Jade Spring Hill and the Garden of Perfect Splendor there was Mt. Wengshan, and that down the hill there was an expanse of water known as the Wengshan Lake. So the emperor ordered construction of one more garden there, presumably as a gift to the queen mother in celebration of her 60th birthday.

Work began in 1750 on construction of the Garden of Clear Ripples. Lake Wengshan was dredged and enlarged, and an embankment, along with a sluice gate, was built on the east bank of the lake. The Wengshan Lake had its name changed into the Kunming Lake. Meanwhile, earth from digging of the lake was piled up on Mt. Wengshan. Going hand-in-hand was construction of pavilions and other structures on the hill. Upon completion of the job, Mt. Wengshan had its name changed into the "Longevity Hill".

The entire project was completed in 1764. The Garden of Clear Ripples, some 290 hectares large, can be divided into three parts. The first part consists of palace structures that we can see immediately after we enter the garden's east gate. As a rule, an imperial abode is invariably fitted with palace halls where the emperor worked on state affairs while staying there. The palace structures in the Garden of Clear Ripples are in a neat group like those in the Forbidden City, but are smaller in size and not as lavishly decorated. The Hall of Benevolence and Longevity, the most important palace structure where imperial audiences were given, lies in the frontal part of the palace complex in following the same ground plan as the Forbidden City. Behind the hall there is the imperial bedchamber, along with buildings designed to serve other imperial needs.

After visiting these palace halls, chambers and courtyards, we find ourselves in the main part of the garden. The Longevity Hill is there, facing south, with a part of the Kunming Lake lying at its foot. Now let's go up the hill. In the middle of the slope we find ourselves in the Temple of Divine Gratitude and Life Prolongation, which comprises buildings in neat groups at different heights of the hill. At either side of the main structures that sit astride the axis of the slope, up the hill, there is a row of other buildings - temples, recreational facilities, etc. Here we are, at the top of the hill, marveling the dazzling beauty of the Buddha Fragrance Pavilion, a structure 40 meters high and glistening with tiles glazed in bright yellow and green.

Down the hill, on the embankment on the west bank of the Kunming Lake, we are now taking a stroll. The embankment is modeled after the Su[4] Embankment on the West Lake in Hangzhou, with six marble bridges counted on it. In the lake we find three islets, symbolizing the three immortals' islands of Penglai, Yingzhou and Fangzhang. At the foot of the Longevity Hill there is the Long Corridor - as long as 728 meters - that extends from east to west, through the breadth of the frontal part of the Garden of Perfect Splendor. Now we are taking one more stroll, in the Long Corridor, enjoying the Kunming Lake and the buildings on the slope of the hill. But, as we walk along, we feel even more fascinated by those colorful pictures done on the beams. Each picture tells a different story, true or legendary, which are told in traditional operas or passed down orally from generation to generation.

Behind the Longevity Hill, at the foot of its north slope, the scenery

The Long Corridor in the Summer Palace.

The Buddha Fragrance Pavilion on the Hill of Longevity.

is no less enchanting even though the place is much smaller. There is a space of just 50 meters in between the foot of the hill and the north wall of the garden. A man-made river, fed by the Kunming Lake, snakes round the foot of the hill, and there are a string of artificial hills along the wall, built with earth from digging of the river. We are now boating on the river, enjoying scenery on either bank, which changes as the rivers widens and narrows. While on the mid-stream, we find, on both banks, rows of old-style shops, again the famous Suzhou Street.[5] Behind the Longevity Hill we are afforded a different kind of visual beauty. The area is so tranquil, and so serene, in sharp contrast to the color and grandeur we have just enjoyed at the other side of the hill.

Like the Garden of Perfect Splendor, the Garden of Clear Ripples was reduced to ruins in the Second Opium War. After the pillage, the only structures that still stood were the marble base of the Buddha Fragrance Pavilion and a few stone structures at the foot of the Longevity

The stream winding at the foot of the north slope of the Longevity Hill.

Structures on the north slope of the Longevity Hill.

Hill. The garden was virtually deserted. So goes a poem by a poet who was able to see the ruins:

> *Sobbing is the Jade Spring, and wailing is the Kunming*
> *The lone bronze bull[6] crouches in thorns overgrown;*
> *Foxes howl in the wilderness, in the dark night*
> *And fish, sleepless, are waiting in vain for the daylight.*

In 1888, Empress Dowager Ci Xi ordered reconstruction of the garden's main parts, and changed the name of the garden into the Garden of Peace and Harmony. The garden was pillaged again, this time by allied forces of eight imperialist powers[7] that stormed into Beijing to suppress the Boxers' rebellion and bring China down on her knees. British, Italian and Tsarist Russian troops were stationed in the garden for a whole year, and they never hesitated to loot those imperial treasures kept there and destroy the structures. In 1902, major repairs were done on the garden. Two years afterwards, Empress Dowager Ci Xi had her 70th birthday celebrated in the garden, and that was the last time that the Qing Dynasty used the Garden of Peace and Harmony or Summer Palace to celebrate a major event. In 1911, the Qing Dynasty was toppled, and China became a republic.

Private Gardens in the South

Like palace structures, private gardens have a long history, developing almost as fast as imperial gardens in the period of Wei-Jin and South-North Dynasties and the following centuries to eventually become an independent branch of the classical Chinese architecture. The best representatives of private gardens built in ancient times are found in parts of Jiangsu and Zhejiang provinces south of the Yangtze River, one of the best-developed regions in the country.

Rivers crisscross and lakes dot this fertile plane, the "Jiang-Zhe area" as it is traditionally referred to. Ever since ancient times, the area has been known for the so-called "lake rocks" — rocks from lakes that are exotic in shape with exquisite lines with which miniature landscapes and artificial mountains and hills are built in gardens and courtyards. Situated in the North Temperate Zone, the Jiang-Zhe area is lush green all the year round, with a mild climate characteristic of the Temperate Zone. Hills are limited in numbers in the area, but their rocks are of a good enough quality to be processed into fine building materials. To sum up, the area is ideal for construction of gardens as far as its natural conditions are concerned.

Ever since ancient times, the Jiang-Zhe area has been referred to as the "land of rice and fish" for its abundance and prosperity. A string of thriving cities emerged as agricultural production and handicraft industry kept developing in the area. Yangzhou, one of them, was China's leading trading port in the Tang Dynasty.

By taking advantage of its economic prosperity, the area was able to gather large numbers of intellectual talents. This in turn boosted the development painting and poetry, which were closely associated with traditional gardening. After the South Song Dynasty (1147-1279) was established with Lin'an (what is now Hangzhou) as capital, large numbers of government officials and merchants from the war-torn north flocked to the Jiang-Zhe area. While rich enough to build residences and gardens for themselves, many of these people were experts of gardening themselves. Gardening continued to thrive in the Ming and Qing dynasties, when the country was unified again. Numerous scholars in the area were able to take official posts in Beijing, the national capital. After retirement, these people would go back to their hometowns, where they would, like their predecessors, build residences and gardens for themselves, and in many cases they would do the designing personally. Ji Cheng (1579-?) of the late Ming period was a most outstanding garden designer the area was able to produce. While a poet, writer and painter, he designed some of the most famous gardens in the area. But he was even better known for his book On Gardening, a summary of gardening in all aspects, ranging from selection of the sites for construction of gardens, use of building materials, building of artificial hills and mountains, to road paving and building of the walls. The book is still valued for a brilliant exposition of traditional gardening as a unique art form.

Characteristics of private gardens:

"Attainment of natural beauty through human labor" was the guiding principle for construction of both imperial and private gardens. But private gardens are different from imperial gardens in many ways. In the first place, private gardens are much smaller, unlike imperial gardens that often occupy several hundred hectares. Private gardens are a part of people's homes and, therefore, are often found in urban centers. In comparison, imperial gardens are found on remote suburbs of the capital city. As the emperor's temporary abode, an imperial garden invariably contains a large complex of palace halls that served the needs of the emperor and his family, including, for example, a hall where the emperor granted audiences to his court ministers. Private gardens, however, were meant for private retreat and as such, were designed to afford a demeanor of urbanity and tranquility. In architectural style, private gardens are simple and refined, suiting the individual taste of their owners, while imperial gardens, even though refined, are magnificent and imposing

Waterside corridor in the Garden of the Humble Administrator, Suzhou.

enough to impress people with the imperial might.

Techniques employed in construction of private gardens:
Though limited in size, classical gardens were designed to meet demanding requirements. There was the need to create a kind of surroundings liable to make people feel as if they were in the natural world. The various structures have to melt into such a surrounding while able to provide sufficient ease and comfort. The studies, in particular, must be quiet. What techniques were used to ensure that such requirements were to be met?

In the first place, minute attention was paid to the distribution of the various structures in a garden to make it beautiful with a variety of scenes. As we can see in ancient gardens, a hall, a pavilion or a gaily-painted pleasure boat can constitute an object of visual beauty, so does an old tree, a grove of bamboo, or an artificial hill. While independent of one another, these, linked by a web of winding trails, present a picture

A corner of the Slender West Lake,
Yangzhou City, Jiangsu Province.

A corner of the Garden of Lions, Suzhou, Jiangsu Province.

beautiful with many things that are well spaced and proportioned. Taking a stroll along the trails in such a garden, we can always see something new a few steps ahead. Corridors are indispensable in ancient gardens found in the Jiang-Zhe area where it is hot and rainy in summer. They are winding, the same way as trails. Straight trails and corridors, as a matter of fact, were a taboo to garden designing. Most corridors are built along the walls, either separated from the wall or against it. Gardens on hills invariably feature corridors winding up and down on the slopes. In many cases, corridors extend into the pond in a garden. Corridors often have windows in the shape of a gourd, a lotus flower, etc. which, together with flowers, bamboo groves and pavilions beyond, produce the same visual effect as traditional Chinese paintings.

Secondly, ancient Chinese architects were good at reproducing natural scenes. Take artificial mountains, for example. Artificial mountains could be built either with rocks or earth. But in all cases architect would see to it that on no account must the mountains look like a neat row of sawteeth. Instead, they must look like real mountains, rising and falling on a rolling terrain. Miniature trees would be planted

Beautifully white-washed walls and spacious corridors feature the Garden of Lions.

on such "mountains". Pains were also taken to make the ponds look natural, and never would it do to make the ponds look like swimming pools. Bridges would be built to partition the water surface if a pond was large enough. Lotus flowers would be grown in the pond, but would not cover the entire water surface. Besides, water would be diverted from one corner of the pond to the miniature lake at the foot of the artificial mountain. As we have already stated, attainment of natural beauty in things built by human labor is the overriding principle for design and construction of gardens in traditional Chinese style.

Thirdly, minute attention was paid to architectural details. This principle had to be followed because private gardens left over from the past are always limited in size, thus allowing a close view of everything. Take the doors and windows, for examples. Doors differ from one another in shape - rectangular, octagonal or in the shape of the full moon or a plum flower. Like the doors, every window is an artwork with exquisite designs and in exotic shapes. On windows in ancient gardens in Suzhou, more than 100 different designs are counted.

Moreover, doors and windows in traditional Chinese gardens, whether of bricks or timber, always feature decorative borders. The surface of the ground is often paved with carefully selected pebbles or bricks, in such a way as to form a variety of designs. Even though the bricks are close against one another, grass is planted in between them to make the designs livelier. Exotic rocks are used to build artificial mountains with, but more often than not, one single rock can be made into a landscape in miniature.

These and other techniques were also used in construction of imperial gardens and, in many cases, some of the best-known private gardens

A courtyard in the Garden of Lions.

A hall in the Lingering Garden, Suzhou.

were copied or modeled after. One example is the Garden of Harmonious Delight, one of the gardens within the Summer Palace, which is modeled after the Garden for Ease of Mind in Wuxi, Jiangsu Province. The best-known private gardens represent the essence of China's traditional architectural art, though not necessarily the highest architectural achievements made in ancient China. Many of these gardens are recognized worldwide for their historic and artistic importance, including the Garden of Lingering, Garden of the Humble Administrator and Garden of Lions in Suzhou on the UNESCO List of World Heritage.

1.The West Lake in Hangzhou has been one of China's best known scenic spots since ancient times.
2.The "five gardns on three hills" refer to the Garden of Tranquility and Appropriateness on the Fragrance Hill, Garden of Light and Tranquility on the

Jade Spring Hill, and Garden of Clear Ripples, Garden of Pleasant Spring and Garden of Perfect Splendor on the Longevity Hill.

3. These include the Ladle Garden, Garden of Brightness and Garden of Luxurant Green, which are now on the campus of the prestigious Peking University. The Tsinghua University, which is also as reputed as the Peking University, is named after the Tsinghua Garden or Garden of Purity and Freshness.

4. "Su" refers to Su Dongpo (1037-1101), a most famous poet and statesman of the Song Dynasty. Su Dongpo, *alias* Su Shi, organized construction of the embankment to prevent flooding of the West Lake when he served as controller-general of the city.

5. Crisscrossed by rivers, Suzhou is often referred to as the "Venice in China". The city affords a unique landscape with shops, restaurants, etc. lining the winding rivers.

6. The bronze bull on the Kunming Lake supposedly has the magic power to ward off flooding.

7. The eight imperialist powers are Britain, France, Germany, Italy, the United States, Russia, Austria and Japan.

Residential Buildings

Residential buildings represent the basic form of architectural art. In China, residential buildings are diverse in style and structure as natural conditions and folkways differ from place to place and from one ethnic group to another. Plateaus and mountains account for a large part of western China. In comparison, the coastal east is largely flat. Vast expanses of desert and grassland feature most parts of north China. The central south, however, is hilly. The country is so large that it covers, from north to south, the Cold Temperate Zone, Mild Temperate Zone, Warm Temperate Zone, Subtropical Zone and Tropical Zone. When north China is covered with snow, the Hainan Island on the southern tip of the Chinese Mainland remains lush green with topical plants.

Sketch of a typical si he yuan in Beijing.

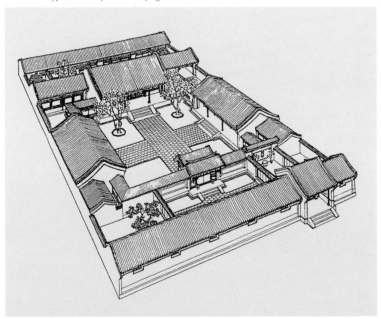

The inner courtyard of a si he yuan in Beijing.

Traditional residential buildings are always built with locally available materials — bricks, timber, bamboo, stone, etc. Here is a brief account of the different types of residential buildings in China:

Si He Yuan in North China

In north China, *si he yuan* are the most popular housing buildings in traditional style. A *si he yuan* is a rectangular compound with traditional one-story houses of gray tiles and bricks built on the four sides of it. The most typical *si he yuan* compounds are found in Beijing.

Buildings in a typical *si he yuan* are arranged in neat rows on the four sides of the compound — the east, west, north and south, which are linked by verandas. The main rooms, which face south and are the largest and brightest, are reserved for the seniors, while the juniors live in rooms of the east and west rows. Facing the main rooms, in the south, is a veranda with a gate — the "inner gate" — in the middle.

Inside this "inner gate" lies the "inner courtyard", the living quarters of the family or the main part of the compound. The "outer courtyard", often rectangular in shape, lies beyond the "inner gate". Facing the "inner gate" is a row of buildings reserved for male servants and guests. The building at the east end of the row, however, is the main gate of the compound. Female helpers live in a small courtyard at the far end of the "inner courtyard", where there are also kitchens and storerooms. Rooms flanking the main rooms are used as toilets. The compound would have been totally enclosed but for the main gate, while doors and windows are invariably open inwardly, obviously to ensure peace and privacy of the family. While serving the needs of family members, the compound enlivens those patriarchal rules that calls for an explicitly defined order of the senior and the junior, the master and the servant, and those belonging to the family and those who do not.

Now let's get into the compound, through the main gate. The first thing that greets our eyes is a screen wall of bricks with decorated patterns. Our guide tells us that in many compounds, potted flowers or exotic rocks are found before the screen walls. By courtesy of our host, we are allowed into the "inner courtyard", which turns out to be a pleasant garden with painstakingly pruned plants. We are told that many

A si he yuan in Jincheng, Shanxi Province.

The gate of a si he yuan in Jincheng, Shanxi Province.

si he yuan compounds are alive with plants in three seasons of the year
— pear or peach trees that bloom in Spring, willows that provide shade
in Summer, and persimmon or date trees that bear fruit in Autumn.
Even though the space is limited, we find two roads forming a neat
cross in the middle of the courtyard. Such roads, we are told, can be
paved with either pebbles or bricks.

Si he yuan compounds can be large or small, depending on the social status and financial capabilities of their owners. A *si he yuan* can be very small and crowded, a simple courtyard occupied by several or even scores of families. A large, rich family with three or more generations "living under the same roof" may, however, own a mansion consisting several *si he yuan* compounds standing side by side or one after another, often with a family garden. Sandwiched in between two rows of *si he yuan* compounds, large or small, is an alley, or *hu tong* as known to Beijing residents. Both ends of the *hu tong* are connected with busy streets. Look at an old map of Beijing you'll find the entire city cut into neat blocks by webs of *hu tongs*, each block being a residential area. Beijing is rapidly modernizing, and many old *si he yuan* compounds are gone, along with numerous *hu tongs* that have been widened. Tours of the remaining *hu tongs* on a rickshaw are becoming popular, reminding people of those long, long years when *hu tongs*, long or short, narrow or relatively wide, were alive with small traders hawking their goods including even "sweet water"[1], or buying secondhand clothing for resale. The centuries-old *hu tong* culture cries for preservation. Let's hope for the best.

Si he yuan can also be found in northeast China, but are different in style and ground plane from those in Beijing. Winter is long and cold in this area, where the population density is relative small. Besides, horse-drawn carts are the chief means of transportation in the countryside. A typical *si he yuan* there is large, with a gate wide enough for a horse-drawn cart to get in and out. The compound is rectangular in shape, with the north side much longer than the east and west sides, so that more south-facing buildings can be built for sunshine in winter.

In old times, Shanxi Province in north China produced some of China's richest merchants, who invariably had residences built in cities. The compounds, some of which have been preserved to this day, are similar to *si he yuan* in Beijing. A typical Shanxi compound is a neat square, enclosed by four neat rows of buildings and with the gate at the east end of the north-facing outermost row. But, unlike a Beijing *si he*

Riverside houses in a south Anhui village.

yuan formed by one-story structures, most structures enclosed in a typical Shanxi compound are two-story buildings and, in many cases, the principal building occupied by the most senior elder of the family is three stories high. The gate often has an elaborately decorated arch over it. At either side of the gate there is a fierce-looking stone lion supposedly to ward off evil spirits. Also found outside the gate is a stone drum that serves as the base for a high pole. Like the stone lions, the pole is a symbol of the family's might. To sum up, Shanxi compounds look more imposing and majestic than *si he yuan* in Beijing.

Tian Jing Courtyards in Southern China

We are now giving an account of residential buildings in Jiangsu, Zhejiang, Anhui and Jiangxi provinces on the lower reaches of the Yangtze River. A typical courtyard there is formed with buildings on four sides, or with buildings on three sides and a wall on the remaining side. These areas are densely populated and land is precious. Therefore, courtyards, or *tian jing* ("heavenly wells") as known to local people,

A village in south Anhui Province.

Brick carvings atop the gate of a residential compound in south Anhui.

are small and most structures in them are two stories high. With multistory buildings on all or the rear, left and right sides of it, a *tian jing* courtyard does look like a well or a chimney, which is meant to prevent the scorching sun from slanting in directly and allows sufficient ventilation. The yard receives water discharged from the rooms. This practice may be linked to the old tradition summarized as "letting no rich water flow into other families' fields". Moreover, the yard is often fitted with exterior fireproof walls. These walls, which are high enough to overlook the buildings in the yard, are whitewashed while the top is built of bluish black tiles, thus forming a pleasant contrast.

In most cases, the principal building in a *tian jing* courtyard consists of three rooms, or up to five or even more if the family is rich. The room in the middle, or the principal room, is the largest. It is the venue of family meetings and also serves as the drawing room. Rooms at either side of the principal room are reserved for the head of the family and his eldest son, respectively. The side rooms, rooms that flank the principal building, are for other children or used as storerooms. A large, rich family may have a large compound consisting of several interconnected *tian jing* courtyards.

In Suzhou, "China's Venice", residential structures are often built at the side of rivers that run parallel to streets, or are connected with streets by bridges. The city lies in the center of the Takhu Lake Valley, the "region of lakes and rivers", where water is often diverted into villages or right into courtyards. Boating along these winding rivers through towns and villages in the area will be a wonderful experience, an experience that one will never forget.

"Seal Courtyards" in Yunnan

Yunnan Province in southwest China neighbors Myanmar, Laos and Vietnam, and is green all the year round thanks to a subtropical or tropical climate. Residential buildings similar to *si he yuan* can be found in central Yunnan. A typical courtyard in the area is a neat square — a "seal courtyard" as local people call it. The principal building in a "seal courtyard" is a three-room structure, and is flanked at either side by a two-room structure. Opposite the principal building there is a neat row of structures, with the gate of the "seal courtyard" in the middle. All the structures are two-story buildings, and the walls facing the streets are high and, in most cases, without windows. The middle room on the first floor of the principal structure is reserved for guests, and the rooms at either side of it are the family's bedchambers. The middle room on the upper floor, however, is for Buddha or ancestral worshipping ancestors. Among *si he yuan*-like courtyards found in China's deep south, "seal courtyards" are the most compact in structure.

In the picturesque Dali where a dozen ethnic minority groups live, courtyards assume a variety of forms. There are courtyards formed with three rows of structures with a screen wall facing the principal building. The screen wall is whitewashed, on which colorful pictures are done, adding beauty to the courtyard while making it brighter. There are also courtyards enclosed in four structures. What is peculiar is that

A typical si he yuan in traditional style of the Bai ethnic group. The photo was taken in Dali, Yunnan Province.

at each corner of a courtyard there is a smaller courtyard — so "five courtyards enclosed by four buildings", as local people put it. Though different in ground plan, courtyards of the two types have a lot in common in architectural style with distinct ethnic characteristics. These courtyards are pretty large. The roofs, built with tiles, are beautifully shaped with the tips bending upwards. Minute attention is paid to exterior decoration of the buildings, which are mostly structures of timber. The walls are always carefully whitewashed, with a decorative border round on the upper parts. Mainly in black and white, the border forms a pleasant contrast. But it is the gate and the screen wall that receive the utmost attention. At either side of the gate there stands a column. Beams supported by the columns form a multi-story structure, with a set of brackets on its top. Colorful pictures and designs are painted on the beams and brackets, which fit so perfectly with the pure white walls. Ethnic Bais like to compare their residential buildings to beautiful girls who is in pure white trousers and jackets while wearing a head

Cave dwelling in north Shaanxi Province.

gears elaborate in design and bright in color.

Cave Dwelling in Northwest China

Cave dwellings constitute a unique scene in the cold, dry loess highlands of northwest China that encompass parts of Shanxi, Shaanxi, Henan and Gansu provinces. Earthen slopes there are solid enough to be dug in, in part because rain is scarce.

Cave dwellings fall into two major types. There are those built by tunneling into an earthen slope. A typical cave dwelling of this kind is a rectangular "tunnel" with a vault-like top and a door and a window at the opening. The "tunnel", so to speak, is up to eight meters deep and three or four meters in width and height. A family may occupy one cave or several standing side by side on the same slope. In some cases, the caves occupied by a family are connected with one another from inside. If the slope is high and solid enough, the family often has two or more layers of caves dug on it. Buildings are often seen in front of a cave dwelling, which are walled to form a *si he yuan*-like courtyard.

There are also "underground cave dwellings" or "underground

compounds". In constructing a cave dwelling of this kind, people dig a deep well — usually seven or eight meters deep and up to 15 meters wide — on a piece of flatland, and then dig into the walls of the well for space to live in. Meanwhile, flowers are grown in the bottom of the well. "Barking of dogs can be heard but no human being can be seen" - this old saying is a vivid description of those underground compounds.

Cave dwellings of both types are cost effective in construction while able to afford sufficient comfort all the year round, cool in summer and warm in winter. Poor ventilation and humidity are the chief defects. If

Cave dwelling in north Shaanxi Province.

not strong enough, cave dwellings may collapse in downpours.

Tu Lou compounds

Of the residential buildings of all types found anywhere in China - maybe anywhere in the world, *tu lou* compounds found in parts of Fujian and Guangdong on the Chinese coast are probably the most unique in construction style and structure. A *tu lou* compound is home to scores of families belonging to the same clan. Seen from a distance, *tu lou* compounds, cone-shaped or rectangular, look like castles. A *tu lou* compound is enclosed by a round wall of rammed earth up to two meters thick and as tall as a four- or five-story building, with a few window-like holes dug through its upper part. This phenomenon, which is not to be found elsewhere in the world, is attributed to wars in ancient times that forced people in the north to flee to Fujian, Guangdong and other parts of China's deep south. The immigrants, known as "Hakkas"

Sectional drawing of a tu lou compound in Fujian Province.

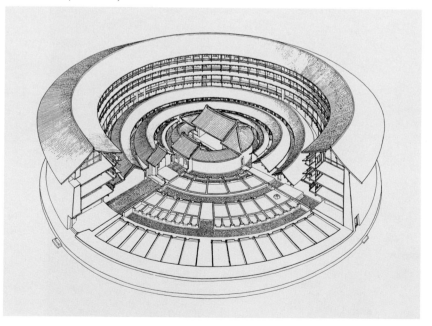

ARCHITECTURAL ART OF ANCIENT CHINA

A tu lou compound in Fujian Province.

or "guest people", were not to live in peace, as clashes with natives were common occurrences due to cultural and psychological differences and conflicting interests. In order to survive, families of a Hakka clan had to live together and, as time went by, learned to build those castle-like *tu lou* compounds for self-defense. But thanks to this, their ancient clan culture and folkways have been preserved to this day.

Cone-shaped *tu lou* compounds interest visitors more than those rectangular in shape. A cone-shaped *tu lou* compound of the average size is somewhere between 50 and 60 meters in diameters, but there are still larger ones with a diameter as great as 90 meters. Let's have a look at the Chengqi Compound at Yongding County, Fujian Province, a typical *tu lou* compound built in mid-Qing period. The compound, 62 meters in diameter, is surrounded by walls as high as ten meters. Buildings inside the compound form three enclosures, one within another, which together have more than 300 rooms. The innermost enclosure, where the clan's ancestors are worshipped, is the venue of meetings, weddings and funerals. The outermost enclosure turns out to be a four-story cone-shaped building. Rooms on the first floor are used

as kitchens and storerooms. Food grain is stored in rooms on the second floor. The third and four floors are the living quarters of the families.

As we have mentioned, *tu lou* compounds were initially meant for self-defense, hence their thick, strong outer walls — one to 2.5 meters thick and of rammed earth strengthened with lime. Such walls became increasingly strong and hardened as time went by, so strong that some have withstood bombardment without collapsing. Even stronger is the foundation of the walls which, in most cases, is built with large pebbles, so that the enemy finds it impossible to tunnel into the compound through it. All windows are open inwardly. Meanwhile, there are bullet holes on the upper part of the outer walls. *Tu lou* compounds have few gates despite their huge size. The Chengqi Compound, for example, has only three. The gate frames are built with stone. The gates are of strong timber wrapped in iron sheets, which are supported by bolts crossing behind them. Water tanks are often found atop the gate — a precaution against enemy attempt to set fire to the building. With sufficient grain and other supplies in reserve as well as water wells inside of it, the compound could withstand a prolonged siege.

Houses on Raised Platforms

People of ethnic minority groups inhabit areas in China's deep south and southwest, mostly in rainy, hot mountains areas in Guangxi, Hunan, Guizhou and Yunnan. For ventilation and for protection from animals and harmful insects, they prefer to live in houses on raised platforms built with locally available materials. In southeast Guizhou where people of the Dong and Miao ethnic groups live in rugged mountains, houses have to be built on slopes and with timber. A typical house is usually built on a raised platform without walls. The part below the platform is used as the family's animal shed or storeroom. Rooms for the family and guests, however, are on the platform. For more space round the rooms, the platform may be enlarged.

The drum tower in a Dong ethnic
village, Guizhou Province.

Almost every Dong village has a drum tower in its center. It is a pyramid-like multi-story structure of timber, and is square, hexagonal or octagonal in shape with colorful human and animal figures painted on the eaves. Villagers gather in front of the tower for gala parties on festival occasions, and for gossiping and information sharing after supper every day. The drum atop the tower will be beaten to call villagers for impromptu meetings. Tea is provided in the tower for free. In winter, the tower is heated inside with charcoal fire.

The Dais in Yunnan Province lives in areas where bamboo groves thrive, hence their "bamboo huts" built on platforms of bamboo tilts. Bedrooms and guestrooms are on the platform, while the space under the platform is used as animal sheds or storerooms. Thick bamboo trunks are used to construct the roof trusses. A typical "bamboo" hut has a straw roof, and its walls are in fact bamboo mats. It is rectangular in shape, its superstructure consisting of several rooms. The principal room is in the middle which, with a fire pan in the center, is the family's kitchen and meeting place. The family has meals outside the principal room, under its eave. Laundry is done on the flat roof, which is also the

A village of the Miao ethnic minority group in south Guizhou Province.

A typical Dai-style house in the Jinghong Prefecture, Yunnan Province.

place for airing grain.

Stone Houses

Stone houses are popular in Tibet, western Sichuan and parts of Qinghai and Gansu in western China, where ethnic Tibetans live in compact communities. A typical stone house is a three-story structure. The ground floor is used as animal shed, and the second floor, as the family's living quarters. The top floor, however, features the family hall for Buddha worshipping. A well-to-do urban family often has a courtyard, with a row of two-story buildings at each of the four sides.

A Tibetan-style house.

The bedrooms, kitchens and guestrooms are on the first floor, the family hall for Buddha worshipping, on the upper floor. The hall for Buddha worshipping is always the most importance place whether the house is large or small and wherever it is, in an urban center or in the countryside. And as such, it is always richly decorated. The lower part of the structure is built with rocks without polishing, and the upper part is painstaking whitewashed. Ladder-shaped windows in neat rows constitute a salient feature of such a structure, and all the window eaves are painted in bright colors.

Yurts and Tents

Ever since ancient times, ethnic Mongolian nomads have lived on grasslands of Inner Mongolia, roving about in search of water and grass for their animal herds. Yurts, also known as "Mongolian tents", are their mobile homes, which are easy to strike for transport and reassemble. A typical yurt is round, about two meters high and four to six meters in diameter, in fact a web of wooden beams and bars covered all over with felt. It has an opening at the top to admit in air and light,

Khazak tents.

Inside a Khazak tent.

and a stove in the middle for cooking and heating. Inside the yurt, the ground is carpeted, and the walls are gaily decorated with tapestries.

Tents used by ethnic Khazak nomads in Western Xinjiang are much the same. The difference is that the felt covering the lower part of a Khazak tent can be rolled up for light and ventilation.

1. Old Beijing had no waterworks. Drinking water, or "sweet water", had to be carted in from the Western Hills. For washing, people used water from wells in the city center - "bitter water" as it tasted bad.